Pictures from the Past

Memories, milestones and everyday life from America's family album

Table of Contents

5   **INTRODUCTION**

6   **CHAPTER 1:** GROWING UP
Return to the carefree days when youth, we were certain, was eternal. Recall the toys and games that amused us, life lessons learned, the excitement that came with each new season and the loyal friends who eased our growing pains.

32   **CHAPTER 2:** ON THE ROAD
Cruising in that hard-earned first car, burning rubber in a souped-up Chevy, packing up the family station wagon for a cross-country vacation—all of these experiences put you in the driver's seat on a freewheeling trip down memory lane.

52   **CHAPTER 3:** ROMANCE
There's nothing like a good love story, as these engaging photographs of teen crushes, college sweethearts, newlyweds and married couples beautifully illustrate—from a shy "hi" to happily ever after.

72   **CHAPTER 4:** HOME SWEET HOME
If you're looking for the joy of day-to-day moments, there's no place quite like home to find it. From big-city apartments to farmsteads and suburban backyards, home's the perfect backdrop for unforgettable photos.

92   **CHAPTER 5:** FUN & GAMES
Cheering on the home team, dancing the tango, fishing for the "big one," riding every ride the midway has to offer—when you're doing the things you love, there's no telling what fun will develop.

112   **CHAPTER 6:** AT WORK
With a can-do attitude and a little elbow grease, almost anything is possible. Get some on-the-job training through the words and pictures of plucky entrepreneurs, tenacious sales ladies, tireless tradesmen and even a lion tamer, all of whom turned their daily labors into love.

132   **CHAPTER 7:** TRUE PATRIOTS
The war years come clearly into focus in the pages of many family albums. Some cameras went off to serve with soldiers, sailors, airmen and Marines, while others remained behind to record the patriotic contributions of folks on the homefront.

152   **CHAPTER 8:** POP CULTURE
Ready for a blast from the past? Open our time capsule of fads, fashions, showbiz glitz and glamour...recall movie heartthrobs, TV stars, big boppers and rockers...and share chance meetings with celebrities that just might leave you starstruck.

168   **CHAPTER 9:** HOLIDAY SPIRIT
From New Year's Day through Christmas, a host of holidays and celebrations offer one photo op after another. Snaps of egg hunts, birthday parties, trick-or-treaters and family feasts are apt to conjure images of your own special traditions.

192   **CHAPTER 10:** JUST FOR FUN
Seriously...some of the most priceless pictures are also the most hilarious. Good-natured pranks, preposterous poses, cute kids and comical pets are guaranteed to make you smile and look on the bright side.

EDITORIAL

EDITOR-IN-CHIEF Catherine Cassidy
CREATIVE DIRECTOR Howard Greenberg
EDITORIAL OPERATIONS DIRECTOR Kerri Balliet

MANAGING EDITOR/PRINT & DIGITAL BOOKS Mark Hagen
ASSOCIATE CREATIVE DIRECTOR Edwin Robles Jr.

EDITOR Amy Glander
ASSOCIATE EDITORS Sharon Selz, Leah Wynalek
ART DIRECTOR Raeann Sundholm
LAYOUT DESIGNER Catherine Fletcher
EDITORIAL PRODUCTION MANAGER Dena Ahlers
COPY CHIEF Deb Warlaumont Mulvey
COPY EDITORS Dulcie Shoener, Joanne Weintraub
EDITORIAL SERVICES ADMINISTRATOR Marie Brannon
EDITORIAL BUSINESS MANAGER Kristy Martin
EDITORIAL BUSINESS ASSOCIATE Samantha Lea Stoeger

EXECUTIVE EDITOR, *REMINISCE* Courtenay Smith
MANAGING EDITOR, *REMINISCE* Kerrie Keegan

BUSINESS

VICE PRESIDENT, PUBLISHER Russell S. Ellis

© 2015 RDA Enthusiast Brands, LLC
1610 N. 2nd St., Suite 102, Milwaukee WI 53212-3906

International Standard Book Number: 978-1-61765-424-4
Library of Congress Control Number: 2014951322
Component Number: 117300045H

IT'S A SNAP...

Anyone who's stumbled across a dusty shoebox full of snapshots knows the feeling. One look at an old photo and you're speeding off on your first two-wheeler, repeating a nervous "I do," sitting sardined between siblings in the family sedan or spending just one more minute with a loved one you'll never forget. A single photo holds a thousand memories...at least.

With the help of many of our more than 1 million readers, *Reminisce*, America's top-selling nostalgia magazine, has put together a family album that's like none other. *Pictures from the Past* celebrates special moments in life, captured with the flash of a camera.

We've raided baby books for glimpses of childhood and tapped wedding albums for a glance at romance. Of course, we snapped up readers' vacation photos, family portraits, and pictures of cherished pets, old homesteads and brave men and women in uniform.

You're sure to chuckle at candids of fun fads, fashions and pastimes. Plus, you'll find picture-perfect examples of first jobs, lasting friendships and family celebrations when everyone huddled together to say "Cheese!"

These colorful pages—featuring more than 500 photos—also focus on real-life stories from readers that make these images so meaningful. Don't be surprised if you click with picture after picture. They might make you laugh or even shed a tear and, for certain, will inspire you to go find your own family photos as an eye-opening legacy for future generations.

Smile!

The editors of *Reminisce* magazine

FIXIN' TO FLY "At age 3, my dad, Albert Babayco, was already developing a lifelong interest in aviation," says Karen Cates of Sacramento, California. "He loved to 'fly' at full speed down the sidewalks of Sacramento in his beloved 1935 Murray pedal car. We still have the goggles!"

CHAPTER 1

Growing Up

AS FAST AS CHILDHOOD WHIZZES BY, THERE
ARE MAGIC MOMENTS OF INNOCENCE,
DISCOVERY AND WONDER THAT HAPPILY
REMIND US, NO MATTER OUR AGE, WE'RE
STILL KIDS AT HEART

Oh, Baby!

LITTLE ONES SPARK PRIDE AND JOY

TRIPLETS GOT DOUBLE TAKES IN THE 1940S

I was—and am—one of three.

My sisters, Kathy and Barbara, and I were born a little after 4 a.m. on July 15, 1946, in Doctors Hospital in Washington, D.C.

Our parents, Benjamin and Freeda Frank, had no idea they were going to have more than one baby that day, and there was a little shock and some fast work as Dr. George Nordlinger and his nurse delivered us over a two-minute span.

We were kept in an incubator for 2½ months (below), as our combined birth weight was 8 pounds, 10¼ ounces.

Mom had her hands full and enlisted the aid of her two older sisters and her mother from Texas. Dad had to be inventive with his finances, trying to get help with items we needed.

We were Pet Milk and Gerber babies for a year in return for publicity. And at the young age of just 21 months, we became the first triplets to ride on American Airlines (bottom, left).

Growing up, we were often placed in different classrooms to keep our teachers from getting confused. Mom put our names on our clothing or picked distinctive colors for our matching outfits—Kathy, pink; Barbara, yellow;

and me, green or blue.

Every time we moved to a new school, we were always noticed, but we never tried to fool anyone on purpose. We just wanted to form our own personalities.

I remember that at our junior high school in Bethesda, Maryland, our graduating class of more than 500 had 17 sets of twos, although we three were the only triplets.

Our brother, Gary, came 15 years after us. Barbara now lives near Baltimore, Maryland, and Kathy lives in the Dallas, Texas, area.

Our family has truly received multiple blessings!

ELLEN JANISZEWSKI DAGSBORO, DE

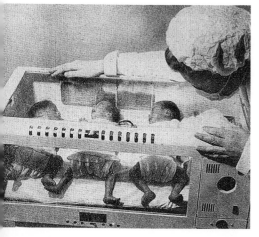

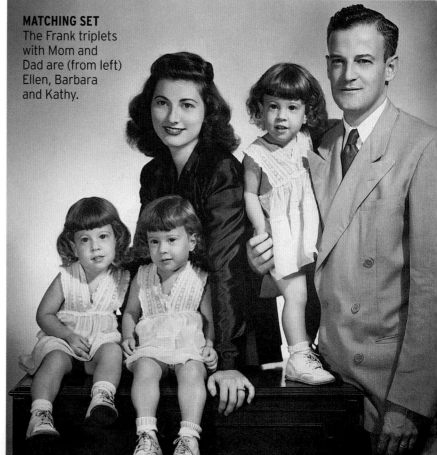

MATCHING SET
The Frank triplets with Mom and Dad are (from left) Ellen, Barbara and Kathy.

JUST DON'T EAT 'EM ➤
"My daughter Lori had just started walking in the spring of '58 and headed straight for these tulips in Roslyn, Pennsylvania," says Virginia Whyte of Ormond Beach, Florida. "Now a grandma, she still loves to smell flowers in her many gardens."

OUT WITH THE BATHWATER? "This picture of my sister Joyce and me was taken in the summer of 1928," writes Donna Gardner Samborn of Auburn, Michigan. "I'm the happy one on the right. We were allowed to cool off in the washtub, half-filled with water, under the supervision of Mother."

"Five years and two more children after this 1950 photo was taken, I enrolled in veterinary college. We graduated in 1962—I earned a DVM, and my teacher wife Evelyn, a PhT, Putting Hubby Through."
STANLEY AGENBROAD EMMETT, ID

THOUGHT TO REMEMBER ~ Each child is a unique and unrepeated miracle.

TAKE A BOW ➤
Little Mike Stehling put on a show in front of the family TV in 1955, says sister Tara Houghton from Dorothy, New Jersey, who shared the adorable picture. At the time, Mike was 2 and the family lived in Fredericksburg, Texas. His dad, Jack, snapped the slide.

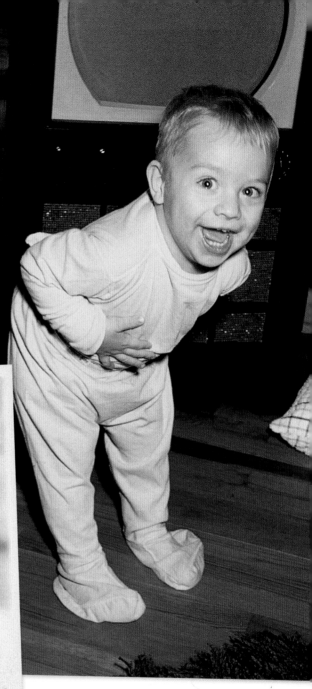

◄ GOT MILK?
"During the '40s, while my husband was in the service, I sent him photos of our daughter, Carole Ann, who was born while he was overseas," writes Rose Ingeson of Glenview, Illinois. "This is one of my favorites. Playing with her milk was more fun than drinking it!"

◄ PEN PALS

"This is my nephew Doug, at 9 months, in '64 in his playpen," says Edith Verda of Granville, Illinois. "I had just changed his diaper and had put him in the pen. Just as I snapped the picture, my little dachshund, Cricket, decided to lap at Doug's face, much to his delight."

▼ HEALTHY BOY

"My husband, Lee, was a large baby, weighing over 10 pounds at birth," says Christina Zimmerman from Junction City, Oregon. "He was already 24 pounds at 7 months in this photo from 1966."

▲ ASPIRING AUTHOR

"I was about 2 years old when I decided to try out the keys on my dad's typewriter," writes Danny Atchley of Mineral Wells, Texas. "I didn't know then that I would go on to publish between 250 and 300 articles and stories, although I collected many rejection slips. Still do!"

Playtime
KIDS ARE GAME FOR ANYTHING

SHIRLEY TEMPLE STYLISH

My twin sister, Carolyn (far left), our older sister, Celia (middle), and I all had our hair done up in Shirley Temple curls for Celia's sixth birthday in 1937; note the cake and presents.

We spent many hours with our coloring books, paper dolls and other projects at that little table, which was usually in the house. We lived on a 1-acre chicken ranch near Santa Barbara, California, and we provided eggs and chickens to a lot of people. We also had goats and a garden.

When trains went by at the back of our property, we'd wave to the engineer and anyone who might be riding in the caboose.

LUCILLE TICO SANTA BARBARA, CA

CELLAR DOORS WERE MADE FOR SLIDING

Seeing my children and their cousins sliding on this old cellar door made me think of the 1940 song "Playmates."

"Playmate, come out and play with me, and bring your dollies three, climb up my apple tree. Look down my rain barrel, slide down my cellar door, and we'll be jolly friends forevermore."

This June 1957 photo was taken at a Beakley family reunion. The reunions have been held annually since the 1930s.

That well-worn cellar door is at the old Beakley homestead near Milburn, Texas, which is still owned by a Beakley.

We're a close family, for sure!

JUNE DRAKE DUNCANVILLE, TX

SWING TIME "Our family had only one income, so we got extras like this swing set for our yard in Newington, Connecticut, by collecting and redeeming S&H Green Stamps," says Peter Arico, who now lives in Rocky Hill. "I encased the post bottoms in concrete for stability, and the kids enjoyed it for many years. Pictured in 1966, from left, are my daughters Jane, age 4, Rona, 6, and Tricia, 1, and their twin playmates, Robert and Ruth Randich."

PAPER OR PLASTIC? "In 1961, it was common to see children playing house, doctor, barber or store," writes Dot Pappas of Irmo, South Carolina. "Our daughter Karen received this store for her birthday and had hours of fun with it. After my husband, Jim, set it in the backyard of our house in Irwin, Pennsylvania, all the children loved to take part in the 'buying' and 'selling.' Those are our sons Robert (at left) and Carl doing some shopping."

HEY BATTER BATTER "Although our son, Stephan, was small for a 7-year-old, he played sports fearlessly," says Norman Schumm, Pittsburgh, Pennsylvania. "His aggressive playing style made him a fan favorite, even for parents from opposing teams. This photo was taken in 1964 in Mount Lebanon, Pennsylvania."

THOUGHT TO REMEMBER ▸ No day is complete until you've heard the laughter of a child.

SLINGS AND ARROWS
Sometimes, all a boy needs for an afternoon of fun is a simple toy. In this photo taken in the 1960s, Lee Turner Jr. watches in wonder as his arrow soars across the sky. His father shared the photo with us.

EARNING HIS WINGS ➤

"When my father worked in the aircraft industry in California, he thought I should have my own airplane to ride," writes Steve Cornell, Nampa, Idaho. "The propeller on this pedal car turned, and Dad installed blinking running lights and put blocks on the pedals so my legs could reach. This photo was taken in Venice in 1953."

DOLL HOSPITAL "My little sister, Mary, plays nurse to a Toni doll in this picture taken by our father, Gene Arneson of Kenosha, Wisconsin, about 1951," says Sara Arneson from Rochester, Minnesota. "After she got a nursing kit for Christmas, she set about caring for all the dolls and stuffed animals in the house. Incidentally, I was the one who became a nurse. Mary recently retired after 39 years as an occupational therapist."

FLOAT OR FLY "Model boats and model airplanes were our son Richard's favorite playthings," writes John Walker of Glen Arm, Maryland. "Here he is with a neighbor friend, Alan, launching his latest model boat on a pond that was near our home in Bel Air. Richard is now a college professor."

"My ingenious dad built us a wooden car in 1961, respectfully named Putt-Nik after the famous Soviet Sputnik satellites and the sound its washing-machine engine made."

JANICE SIMCOE FAIR OAKS, CA

School Days
CLASS PICTURES MAKE THE GRADE

SOME BUNNY TO LOVE

It all started one fall day in 1969 when the janitor of our elementary school in White Sulphur Springs, New York, found a wild baby cottontail rabbit in the schoolyard. Of course, my first-graders fell in love with it and wanted to keep it.

The children named our new "first-grader" Fluffy, and so began a wonderful year for the class. The first child to arrive in the morning opened the cage, and Fluffy would hop out to begin his day.

Fluffy moved around freely, usually until a student picked him up and cuddled him. The class happily wrote stories about him and read to him.

He was their best friend and an ideal classroom pet. He made no noise, didn't bite or scratch and was so soft and cuddly. Best of all, he was trained. Fluffy never had an accident because he always returned to the back of his cage to take care of "business."

Fluffy ate the usual rabbit pellets but quite often he was treated to a leaf of lettuce, a carrot or whatever the children talked their mothers into packing. There was no greater thrill for the children than to have Fluffy join them on their desks for lunch.

He had a very therapeutic effect on the children. One little boy would come in every morning ready to explode. I found that if I could get Fluffy into his arms as soon as he came in, he calmed right down.

One day, a local newspaper reporter visited the school. He was so taken with Fluffy that he took a photo of our class pet planting a kiss on a student, George Worden. That photo ran on the front page of the *Middletown Record*.

Sadly, Fluffy became ill later that year. The *Middletown Record* kindly ran an obituary for him.

Puff the rabbit joined our class next. Then came Penny, who made things more interesting by giving birth to eight bunnies.

At one point, the school district announced there were to be no more classroom pets. When I asked the principal about it, he said, "Mrs. Townsend, if your rabbit is like your past pets, don't pay any attention to that order."

Wouldn't it be nice if teachers today were allowed to be this creative in their classrooms?

ERNA TOWNSEND ADAMS
PINEHURST, NC

TEACHER'S PETS Fluffy gives George Worden, 6, a sweet peck on the cheek during class. This delightful picture ran on the front page of the local newspaper in 1969.

CLASSY BROWN BAGGERS

My father, Donald Jorgensen, took this lunchtime slide (right) in May of 1956. It was just before my friends and I graduated from Washington High School in Sioux Falls, South Dakota, where Dad was a biology teacher.

I am wearing a striped blouse, sitting across the table from Lois Engen Bahnson in glasses, a white blouse and purple skirt.

Most of the students who didn't eat the cafeteria food carried their lunches in brown paper bags. Carrying a lunch box was not cool.

PATRICIA JORGENSEN PALAGI
SEATTLE, WA

"Shiny new pennies always marked the end of the school year for kids in Glenolden, Pennsylvania. After completing third grade in 1944, my classmates and I headed to the street corner where Chief of Police John McVeigh waited to pass out the pennies as a reward for our hard work. It was great to be recognized! I'm the girl front and center with the print dress and the dimples."

LOIS BROWN LEVITTOWN, PA

THOUGHT TO REMEMBER ➤ Teachers open the doors; you enter by yourself.

▲ GRADUATION DAY

"I had my first shampoo and set, which cost 25 cents, for this June 1937 graduation picture of our eighth-grade class at New York Mills Grammar School," writes Lillian Phillips (second row, far left), from Kissimmee, Florida.

SODA STOP ▶

"After school, my mother, Miriam Gaut (right), and her friend Mary Barkley would often stop by Henschen's Drugstore in their small town of Payne, Ohio, to get a Coca-Cola," says Maria Cuney of Grabill, Indiana. "They could order cherry or vanilla flavors, Coke with a peanut in it or just a regular Coke. During the girls' junior high days, my mom got a job as a soda jerk there."

▲ LUNCH BOX KIDS

"On our porch, Douglas and Deborah are headed back to school in 1965, while their sister Ronda is still in her PJs," says mom Elizabeth Dau of Dunnellon, Florida.

◄ THE SKY IS FALLING!

"Our Lowell School first-grade class in Harvey, Illinois, dressed for the play *Chicken Little* in 1915," says John Townsend of Auburn, Alabama. The kids were unmasked for this photo, so we're able to see John, fourth from the left. He played the fox.

SCHOOL CHUMS ►

"I graduated from high school in Mount Iron, Minnesota, with most of the same kids pictured with me in this photo of my first-grade class in 1942," writes Beverly Flankey of Crossville, Tennessee. "Miss Larson was so beautiful, and a wonderful teacher, too. To this day, many of us 38 students from our graduating class remain friends and get together when possible."

▲ AT A CROSSROADS

"Being a member of our school's safety patrol taught us kids responsibility in the good old days," says David Swift, Halifax, Massachusetts (at far left in the back row during a 1950 awards ceremony). "As captain of the patrol boys, I was the envy of the sixth-grade girls."

Friends for Life

SIBLING TIES HAVE NO RIVAL

THE BATTLE OF THE BIKE

The Big Trike was one sweet ride. I still remember when it arrived at our house in Milwaukee in the 1950s: blue with white pinstripes, a red seat and a front wheel twice the size of a normal tricycle wheel. It rode like the wind; no one in our entire neighborhood could beat it in a race.

My tomboy sister, Elizabeth, who was 18 months older and beat me at everything, considered the Big Trike hers just because it arrived around her seventh birthday. But I knew the trike was meant to be shared. That spelled trouble, because she and I defined the term sibling rivalry. In fact, whenever Ma wasn't around, I called her "Lazy Lizzie Lizard."

One day, I decided it was my turn to ride the Big Trike. But no matter how hard I tried, I couldn't pry the Lizard's hands off the handlebars.

So I implemented Plan B. I figured if I blocked the narrow sidewalk along the side of our house, the Lizard would have

to stop and go get Ma. (We didn't dare ride on Pa's lawn.) Then I'd hop on the Big Trike and ride until dinner—that is, if I even got any. It seemed worth the risk.

So, genius that I was, I lay down on my back, across the sidewalk. About 30 seconds later, the Lizard came blasting down the walk. It almost seemed as though she picked up speed when she saw the human speed bump ahead, but I wasn't worried; I knew the Big Trike could stop on a dime.

Then, *whump*! The front wheel ran over my stomach. Now stopped in her tracks, the Lizard ran inside the house to get Ma, just as I'd figured she would. I, however, found myself stuck, wedged between the front and rear wheels.

When Ma came outside to free me, guess who got punished, the innocent pedestrian or the reckless driver? But as it turned out, I didn't want supper anyway—I already had a tummy ache.

JERRY WESSEL MCKEES ROCKS, PA

FREEWHEELING TRIO
Jerry savors a moment on the Big Trike with sisters Liz (left) and Ruth. He drove a smaller set of wheels (above, left) before graduating to the prized Big Trike.

DOORSTEP DREAMS From left, Rose, Anna and Catherine Ferrara pose on their front steps in Brooklyn in 1943 with their parents and in 1946 alone.

FUN AND GAMES ON THE FRONT STOOP

I was lucky to grow up in a lovely brick six-family house on Wyckoff Avenue in Brooklyn, New York, back in the 1940s. Our building was the only one on the block with an ornate iron fence and a large stoop.

Maybe you're not sure what a stoop is. It's simply a step or a series of steps leading up to a platform in front of the door to the house.

But to me, the stoop meant so much more. It meant freedom with a sense of security. My loving parents were very protective of their three young girls, so we weren't allowed outside alone except when we stayed on the stoop. It was a safe haven for us and our friends.

We imagined flying on magic carpets or sailing the high seas on pirate ships. We played games, picnicked, cut out paper dolls and shared our dreams and secrets. The broad top of the stoop served as a stage for dancing and singing to our all-time favorite Betty Grable musicals.

If we sat there long enough, the whole neighborhood would eventually pass by. The sound of high heels clicking meant Mrs. Schembeck running by to catch her train. She'd leave the most delicious smell of lily-of-the-valley trailing behind her.

"Shellshock" Jimmy stomped on all the cellar doors, George rode by on his bike and a scary woman with two sons would walk past, all of them dressed in black.

Invisible but just as memorable was the wonderful scent of freshly baked bread wafting to us from Sollano's Bakery three doors away.

When we were older, boys were allowed to sit with us. They occasionally held our hands, and sometimes they'd even steal a kiss.

Years later, when I was able, I wanted to buy the property and buildings where we lived to help keep all those memories intact, but it was not to be.

Around the block on St. Nicholas Avenue was a little hospital. Over the years, its board began buying up the surrounding property. Finally, almost 50 years after we lived there, the houses on our block were demolished.

Wyckoff Heights Medical Center now dominates our old neighborhood. Our stoop is gone, but I'll never forget all the memories we made there.

CATHERINE FERRARA ZOIDA
HOWARD BEACH, NY

THOUGHT TO REMEMBER ➤ Siblings are the chocolate chips in the cookies of life.

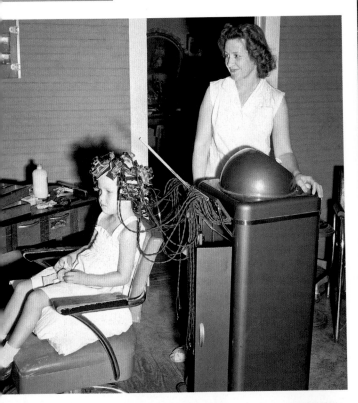

THREE "DAVYS" "Growing up in the '50s, our sons (left to right), Don, 5, Jim, 7, and Rob, 3, enjoyed Walt Disney's *Davy Crockett* television program and the coonskin caps," writes Mary MacLean of Palm Coast, Florida. "The slide was taken in front of our house in Bergenfield, New Jersey. The boys were on their way to the playground."

CURL POWER "A friend of our mother's gave my sister Cheryl and me back-to-school perms in 1952 or '53," says Carol Thompson of Glendale, Arizona. "That's Cheryl looking a little bit frazzled in the chair with her tresses connected to an electric permanent wave machine. I'm on the left in the photo of the two of us showing off our finished results."

HOOK, LINE AND SUPPER "After fishing on the Allegheny River during vacation around 1948, my brother, Rick (left), and I proudly hauled back our catch. Mother obligingly cooked our fish for dinner that evening."

SHARING GRANDMA

For two weeks every July, my parents rented a small cottage in Ontario at Sauble Beach on the eastern shore of Lake Huron.

This photo was taken there in 1959, when I was 3 years old and my brother, Stephen, was about to turn 1. We're sitting with our grandmother Hildegarde Bardon.

I don't appear to be very happy, maybe because my bangs were cut short. It's more likely that I wasn't pleased about being squeezed in beside Grandma instead of on her lap.

Grandma always wore two pairs of glasses in the summer—her regular prescription glasses and what she called her "dark glasses" on top. It was her version of clip-ons.

I often think back on those carefree days at the beach and the cherished family memories we made.

HEATHER BARDON EULER
WATERLOO, ON

"DON'T TOUCH!"
"My sisters, Frances (left) and Shirley, weren't fazed by those words in 1941, with both of them falling under the spell of some dry ice," says Peggie Kamm Bergantino of Northford, Connecticut. "The picture was taken in West Haven, Connecticut."

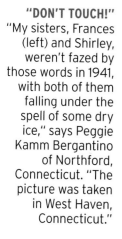

Seasons of Fun
LIFE'S A YEAR-ROUND PLAYGROUND

ONE VERY HAPPY CAMPER

My friend Glenn Aldinger and I were only children in 1956. We had to depend upon school for playmates, so it could be lonely when school let out. Naturally, when the idea of summer camp came up, we jumped at the chance to spend two weeks with other boys.

There was enough open space at Camp Meacham in Kentucky to play games without worrying about running through someone's garden or knocking something off a shelf. There was even enough space for an archery range! We certainly could not shoot a real bow and arrow back home in our Cincinnati neighborhood.

I learned to swim at camp, but not very well. During swim races, I usually came in dead last. But I was never the rotten egg when it came to our favorite camp game. The counselors would toss a greased watermelon into the swimming pool, where it floated for a few seconds. When the whistle blew, all the boys jumped into the pool to try to get it out. The winning cabin got to eat the watermelon.

We called the remote bathroom "Egypt." I remember being frightened by campfire stories about the Ooglie Moog, the monster who lived in the hills south of the camp. I sure made the trip to and from Egypt as quickly as possible at night.

Camp Meacham didn't offer as many activities as summer camps do today. But there was so much to do during the summers of 1956 and 1957 that I didn't have time to get homesick.

R. DAVID POGGE RIDGECREST, CA

SUMMER SCHOOL David (front row, second from right) learned independence and teamwork at Camp Meacham. The boys shared cabin duties (middle) and a fear of meeting the mythical camp monster on trips to the distant bathroom (right).

COOL COUSINS "In 1961, this was our favorite way to cool off–with Popsicles!" writes Kristen Spilman from Ventura, California. "A swing set and a plastic pool were also big helps. Pictured, from the left, are my sister Karen, age 4; cousin Mike, 4; cousin Jimmy, 8; me, 3; and my older brother, Kenny, 8."

CHEERFUL EARFULS "My dad, Art Krueger, liked to grow some fun things like Indian corn and castor beans in his garden in West Allis, Wisconsin," says Kathryn Ridder of Chilton. "The kids having fun are (from left) my brother Kevin (partially hidden), our neighbors David and Patsy, me in the great striped pants and our neighbor Rosie."

RUSTLING UP FUN The Thompson kids (from left), Ann, Robin and Steve, could barely keep their heads above the oak leaves on this October day in 1963. "The picture was taken at a campground in East Troy, Wisconsin," says Bruce Thompson of Waukesha. "We lived in Burlington at the time."

THOUGHT TO REMEMBER ▸ There's a warmth and joy that never ends between the hearts of special friends.

▲ LIFELONG FRIENDS

"After church in Rising City, Nebraska, my sister Melanie and I rushed to Doc Chalquist's house to play with his granddaughters Sue and Deb," writes Dulcie Shoener from Whitefish Bay, Wisconsin. "More than 50 years later, Deb and I are still friends." From left: Melanie, Sue, Dulcie and Deb.

WINTER'S PRETTY SLICK ▶

"On snow days, Mom would gather all the neighborhood kids and our friends in our station wagon and we'd head to Grandma and Grandpa Hurst's farm with sleds and inner tubes," says Kimberly Osborne Townsend from Wheelersburg, Ohio. "I'm in the front of this tube with Jennifer Davis Hayes; Jeff Osborne, Robin Sumner Aleman and Pete Ruby are behind us."

▲ TAKING THE PLUNGE

The swim test is a summer camp tradition and a childhood rite of passage. Lined up on the dock at Camp Minisink in New Jersey in the '50s, these boys are about to become minnows, fish, flying fish or sharks. Ruth Sandow of Longmeadow, Massachusetts, who ran the camp for 10 years, sent in the photo.

◄ SNOW KIDDING

"The winter of 1959-'60 was especially hard in Council Bluffs, Iowa," writes Lu Anne Munyon Kobs of Goltry, Oklahoma. "My dad had trouble keeping the driveway clear, as you can see. I'm on the right, holding the snow clod, with my friends Kathy and Danny Lidget."

SWEET SUCCESS Summer was the best time to have a beverage stand, says Maxine Stenger of Gorham, Maine. "When our daughter, Jill, was growing up in the '60s, she and her friends opened a Kool-Aid stand to raise money for Boston's memorial John F. Kennedy Presidential Library & Museum. Pouring 24 cups at 5 cents apiece from a cold pitcher, Jill and the girls made $1.20. Back then a dollar went a long way."

MUSCLE BEACH "The mighty guys in this 1962 slide are my boys and the sons of two high school buddies," says Ben Hoke, Tulsa, Oklahoma. "The area overlooks California's Antelope Valley."

PICK OF THE CROP Carol Jacobs Norwood grew up in Gardenville, Pennsylvania, where, appropriately, her family's farm was full of fruits and vegetables. "That's me picking raspberries in 1959, when I was 5 years old," writes Carol, who now lives in Myerstown. "We'd eat some raspberries on our cereal, but most of the ones we picked were sold out front at our little produce stand."

HOUSEWARMING "With help from her father and the kids in our Jeffersonville, Indiana, neighborhood, my daughter Barbara Gutkese Robertson built this cozy four-person ice house in 1955," writes Edith Gutkese, who still lives in Jeffersonville. "The girl on the left is Pattie Sue Ryan Powers, Barbara's friend. A rag rug and cocoa kept playtime cozy inside."

SNOWBALL PROTEST "After naughty neighbors knocked our snowman's head off with snowballs for the fourth time, my mother, Anne, organized a protest against snowballs," says Nicole Quandt, Madison, Wisconsin. "Protests were everywhere in Milwaukee in 1969, so we thought we'd join in. Our merry band of protesters included (front row) John Farkas, Cindy Schoening, me and Renee Vanselow and (back row) Kim Farkas, Paul Schoening and Joe Farkas."

WINTER WARRIOR "This is my nephew Erick Brenneman, wanting to get inside our house after a big snowball fight," writes Lois Gugel of Kalona, Iowa. "We lived in the small town of Joetown. Erick's father was a garage mechanic, as was his father before him. They lived just a few miles from us. It's likely Erick came in for dry clothes and went right back out for more fun."

PUCKER UP! "Not even the promise of chocolate milk could get my future husband, Barry, to give this pretty blonde a kiss," says Yvonne Rowley from Montclair, California. The photo was taken for a Shady Grove Dairy ad in 1967.

THE PUBLICITY PARADE

"To capitalize on public interest in the high-performance Corvette, we Chevrolet dealers and managers in Denver arranged to drive a trainload of new cars through the city in August 1957," writes R.R. Shaw, Eagle, Idaho. "We worried about the cars overheating in the mile-high altitude, but we got a lot of publicity and made the cover of the *Chevrolet Dealers News* (right)."

CHEVROLET
DEALERS NEWS

NOT CONNECTED WITH CHEVROLET OR GENERAL MOTORS

AUGUST, 1957

11 Chevrolet Dealers receive Mass Delivery of 36 new Corvettes at Denver, Colorado

CHAPTER 2

On the Road

BUCKLE YOUR SEAT BELTS FOR A JOY RIDE
DOWN LIFE'S HIGHWAY IN SOME CLASSY
VEHICLES THAT PROVE GETTING
THERE'S HALF THE FUN

First Set of Wheels

FINDING THE KEYS TO FREEDOM

LOVED HIS LIMO High-schooler Randy Welborn poses proudly in his first car—a rescued junkyard Cadillac. Although its former owner was a funeral director, the classy Caddy (top photos, opposite) had plenty of life in it.

HE'D RATHER DRIVE A CADDY

When I was 14, I felt as if I was getting too old to ride my bicycle anymore. Back then in the 1950s, it was possible to get a Texas driver's license at age 14. So for one final summer, I rode my bike all the way across town three times a week to take driver's education.

I had my eye on a black '49 Ford convertible at Ralph's Auto Sales, just down the block from my dad's electrical repair shop in Beaumont. But when Dad and I examined the car closely, we found that it had a cracked engine block.

Dad then contacted a friend who had a sort of junkyard/car dealership out behind his home. He had a '41 Cadillac for sale. In fact, it was a limousine!

Dad paid $150 for the car, and I couldn't wait to get home and start fixing it up. It had been painted light blue by the previous owner, a funeral director. Though the car had been used to transport families, my little sister insisted on calling it a hearse.

That Caddy's background didn't bother me a bit. I immediately started work on her interior, refinishing the real wood panels in the doors.

And what an interior my new

vehicle had! It sported two clocks, three glove boxes, five different courtesy lights, two pull-out jump seats and two under-seat heaters (not working).

I couldn't afford all the heater hose required to properly repair those foot warmers. Instead, I rolled up a piece of cardboard like a megaphone, and then jammed it into the defroster outlet so it directed warm air toward my feet.

When I removed the dash clock to clean it, I was surprised to find the words "The Texas Company" written on the back. That meant my car must have been originally owned by Texaco.

For me, this only added to the car's allure—I imagined a bunch of oil tycoons cutting big deals right there in my spacious seven-passenger Caddy!

Now I really wanted to restore my vehicle to its original condition. As the summer wore on, my best friend and I went to work on the car harder than ever.

We planned to finish my car with black lacquer so we could stage a mock gangster shoot-out in front of the Jefferson Theater, right in downtown Beaumont. It would be just like the action we saw on television each Saturday night on *The Untouchables*!

Alas, we could barely scrape up enough money for the gray primer coat, and that's the color the car stayed. But the primer helped earn my Caddy its colorful nickname, Gray Ghost (after the historical Civil War TV series of the mid '50s).

While other teens in town had

ordinary Fords and Chevys (some even new), I was proud to cruise the local drive-ins in my old limo. I even learned how to parallel-park that monster!

Delving into Cadillac history, I learned that the car's flathead V-8 produced 150 hp and that World War II tanks were powered by two of those engines. No wonder my car got only 8 miles to the gallon! Every time I picked up my buddies to cruise around town, I had to pass the hat to collect funds for gas.

Though the car was well-worn and never had anything but bald tires, I was absolutely thrilled to start high school that fall with an auto unlike that being driven by any other kid in town—maybe even the whole country!

My little sister still didn't share my excitement, though. When I drove her to school, she insisted that I drop her off a block away so her friends wouldn't see her getting out of my hearse.

The following spring found my classic Caddy sitting in our yard because I didn't have the money to buy new license plates. The following summer, I met my future wife, and by December, desperate for a nice Christmas gift for her, I made the painful decision to sell my limo to a junk dealer for $20.

I bought my gal an imitation fur coat with the money. We've celebrated many anniversaries since then, so I have no regrets over my investment!

My memories of that car remain especially strong today, because for some reason, the '41 Cadillac limo was a favorite prop in many Hollywood movies, including *Harvey* with Jimmy Stewart.

Often, when I stay up to catch the late show, I can watch my first car in action again—and laugh about the gangland shoot-out that never happened.

RANDY WELBORN KOUNTZE, TX

COLLEGIATE COUPE
"This is me getting into my 1935 Ford V-8 Business Coupe for my daily commute from Chicago to Northwestern University in Evanston, Illinois, where I had just started classes," writes Jerry Feit of Park Ridge. "Dad bought it for me in 1937 for $500. It had hand-painted whitewalls!"

THOUGHT TO REMEMBER ➤ Don't think you're on the right road just because it's a well-beaten path.

◄ POSTWAR PROJECT

"My girlfriend and future wife, Edna, is in the driver's seat of my 1936 Ford convertible with a rumble seat, which I bought in 1947 for $245 after I was discharged from the Marine Corps," writes Thomas Rodgers of Staten Island, New York. "I paid $10 a week until the car was paid off and did all the repair work myself. I kept it for about four years."

RED ROADSTER ►

"I was extremely proud of this sharp 1938 Plymouth Roadster with a rumble seat that I bought as my first car in 1949," says Jim Fonk of Sun Lakes, Arizona. "When I posed with it, little did I know that I'd retire from Chrysler Motors almost 40 years later. What I wouldn't give to take another ride downtown in my little red wagon."

◄ HOT-RODDERS

"This 1948 Chevy convertible was my first car," writes Joyce Hillberry (center) of Lisbon, Ohio. "Mom and Dad gave it to me and my sister, Dorothy, in 1956. She didn't like it because it had a standard shift, but I loved it. The car had spotlights, fog lights and a dual manifold. Could it ever 'lay a strip,' as we used to say in the '50s. Janice Whitacre (left), Marilyn Tullis and I went cruising every weekend."

In 1946, Bob Siegfried (behind the wheel) of Cincinnati, Ohio, and his friend John Chupp (not pictured) purchased this 1917 Model T for $25. The photo was taken that summer at Cornell University in Ithaca, New York, where all four men were employed in the greenhouse at the nutrition lab. They were, or would be, graduates from Cornell. Note the tape on the tired right-front tire and the silly sayings.

▲ NICE HAND-ME-DOWN

"Pictured in 1941 are my brother, Hank Cushard, his brand-new Plymouth convertible and me," writes Anna Staats of Tamarac, Florida. "Shortly after the picture was taken, Hank enlisted in the Air Force and gave his little sister permission to drive the car in his absence. I thought I was the cat's meow."

Mad for Motorcycles

BEST THING ON TWO WHEELS

A 65-YEAR LOVE AFFAIR WITH MOTORBIKES

I was first bitten by the two-wheel bug when I was 14 years old, back in 1947. A friend let me try out his Whizzer, a bicycle with a bolt-on engine that drove the rear wheel. What a thrill!

Next came an ancient Moto-Scoot, found in a farm shed in fixer-upper condition, which I rode until I got a 1947 Salisbury that had been a demonstrator at a small shop in Kent. Built by Northrop Aviation, it was well ahead of its time. I remember riding it to my job as a bowling pin boy the winter of '49. Wearing three sets of gloves, pants, socks and jackets, I still froze.

After entering the service, I did without two-wheelers until 1952, when I came upon a '47 Indian Chief bike in Los Angeles. It's said a man who falls in love with a dimple ends up marrying the whole girl. Well, I loved the look of the Chief's signature fender skirts and bought it.

I traded the Chief for a nimble, saucy Triumph, the first of four I was to have in the '50s. Then, one day in 1955, I stopped in for a part at a Triumph dealership in Venice and saw a sparkling '54 Ariel Square Four 1,000 cc bike. I heard heavenly music, and a voice in my head said, *This is it, boy*!

My new Ariel could break 100 mph with ease and was admired by motorbike enthusiasts everywhere—and respected by the Hawthorne police, who tried on occasion to catch it. A year later, I got married, so the Ariel had to go.

Over the next half-century, I often regretted parting with the Ariel—until, thanks to the Internet, I found its twin in the mountains of Colorado, where it had been rusting for 25 years. Now restored to showroom condition, it's a prized possession and still the most gorgeous machine on the planet.

BILL WARNER PORTERVILLE, CA

DREAM MACHINE
Bill Warner owned many motorbikes, but the 1954 Ariel was his favorite. Bill and wife Ginger both perched on it for photos.

AMERICAN-MADE Cheri Setzer of Milwaukee, Wisconsin, shares this photo of her uncle Henry Setzer working on the Harley-Davidson assembly line at the Juneau Avenue Plant in Milwaukee. The motorcycle was a 1965 Electra Glide.

FREEWHEELIN' DAYS "My mother (far right) is shown circa 1940 with friends on a tour of rural New England," writes William Mahan, West Roxbury, Massachusetts. "She and Dad rode the red Harley."

HARLEY HONEY "Daughter Cheryl loved to wear her brother's cap and boots aboard his scooter in the '50s," says Daisy Henry of Monroe, Michigan.

BEACHCOMBER "Honeymooning in Florida in 1963, we rented this 50 cc Honda motorcycle my wife enjoyed riding on the beach," writes Joe Malhoit, Allen Park, Michigan. "We now have a 1,500 cc Honda Goldwing built for two."

THOUGHT TO REMEMBER ➤ Go any direction in life as long as it's forward.

Our Family Car

C'MON, EVERYBODY PILE IN!

WELCOMING WAGON
Pete's daughter Kate (seated on the hood) gathered the yearbook staff for a photo with Gussy in 1976. Below: Gussy after her high school-friendly makeover.

GUSSY THE GREAT

After graduating from college, I cruised into a Ford dealership ready to swing a deal on a car that would turn heads. I settled on a new '57 Country Sedan Station Wagon with a nine-tube radio and a Thunderbird V-8 292 engine for about $2,700.

My souped-up Ford accelerated my courtship with my girlfriend, Jan, and we married five months later. After a 5,000-mile honeymoon over five states, we loaded up Gussy, as I'd named the wagon, and drove to Phoenix, where a new job awaited me.

We drove each of our four daughters home from the hospital in our faithful wagon, which also saw us through family vacations and teen driving lessons.

After doing yeoman duty for 20 years, Gussy was in need of some care. I did a front-to-rear-bumper renovation for the girls, repainting her fire-engine red and white. The wagon became known on the high school campus as "the fire truck."

We sold Gussy in 1992 for about what I'd paid for her. She was part of a grand experience we will always remember.
PETE JACOBSON PHOENIX, AZ

A BIRD TO BRAG ABOUT Carolyn Langowski of Minocqua, Wisconsin, recalls that she and her husband were the envy of the neighborhood in their 1959 Thunderbird. That T-Bird served them well for 10 years, Carolyn says.

"My uncle Fred Cooper had a canary yellow 1958 BMW Isetta with a front door that hinged open for his nieces and nephews to pile in. Once, we drove the microcar through the snowy mountain roads outside Gatlinburg, Tennessee. I believe my Aunt Blanche gave him what-for for taking me on such a dangerous ride, but I loved it!"

STEVE WHALEY SEVIERVILLE, TN

STILL ON A ROLL

Everyone in our neighborhood in Austin, Texas, wanted a ride in our brand-new 1951 Chevrolet DeLuxe. I was 8 years old when my mom, Lili, got it. More than 60 years later, I'm the one driving that car, which is now firmly entwined in our family history.

I learned a lot while driving in the Chevy with Mom, from hearing the truth about Santa Claus to watching integration protests in Texas. The car became mine when I graduated from high school in 1961 and Mom bought another Chevrolet.

As a graduation present, my grandmother paid to have the green car repainted.

The Chevy took me off to college and then to med school in 1965 in Galveston, where it survived Hurricane Carla and yet another flood where water rose higher than the doors.

In 1966, I met a woman named Judy Lynne while preparing to enter the Peace Corps. On dates, we drove the Chevy on ocean beaches. We got married in 1969, and the Chevy, of course, took us on a trip to Mexico in 1970.

Later, we moved to Chapel Hill, North Carolina, where our first child, Melanie, was born in 1975. She came home from the hospital in the Chevy on a blazing hot summer day.

Our second child, Jennifer, was born in 1978 in Louisville, Kentucky. As we brought her home during a fierce snowstorm, the Chevy got stuck in our driveway. Our third child, Michael, arrived on a spring day in 1981, and the Chevy sported new seat covers for his ride home. (That's our family with Mom and the Chevy at top, and Judy and me in the smaller photo at a car show.)

Now, my grandson, age 3, has taken an interest in the car, which has never been restored and has survived indignities large and small (including an ice storm that caused an accident, and a tree that fell on it). I hope he stays interested—I'd love to keep our old Chevy in the family!

STEVEN LIPPMANN LOUISVILLE, KY

THOUGHT TO REMEMBER ▸ The most important trip you may take in life is meeting people halfway.

FUTURE OWNER
My son, Merrill, went along to the dealership when his grandfather Boyd Fox Sr. ordered this 1965 Ford Falcon Ranchero (above). In this slide from 1967, Merrill was washing the truck on his Easter vacation at his grandfather's farm near Plains, Kansas. Merrill always felt that the Ranchero was his, and today it is.

WARREN PETERSON HUTCHINSON, KS

CRAZY FOR CARS
My dad, John Burke, grew up loving cars, as you can see in this 1927 snapshot (below) of him sitting on the hood of his parents' Hudson. As a young man, he went on to drive for the demolition derby and banged up more than his share of vehicles.

After he married and had children, Dad made a living by driving everything from tour buses and street sweepers to 18-wheelers.

CINDY ANDERSON EDMONDS, WA

LOOK, DAD! NO BUTTONS
My love for the 1961 Oldsmobile Dynamic 88 dates back to that year. My parents bought this model when I was 3. That's my sister Patricia and me (above) in front of the Olds in 1962.

I was fascinated with the car's speedometer. It changed colors as the car went faster, and I always studied the speedometer when my dad was driving.

One time, Dad was stopped for speeding. He tried to explain to the police officer that he could not have been going that fast.

"Yes, you were, Daddy," I piped up from the backseat. "I was watching the speedometer."

Dad got a speeding ticket. It was not funny then, but the story never fails to get laughs at family gatherings.

I always told my parents never to get rid of the car, as I wanted it when I grew up. But in 1969, they sold it for $200 and bought an Olds Delta 88.

Thirty years after we got our first Olds Dynamic 88, I finally was able to buy my own. My boys didn't share my enthusiasm for the speedometer. But they liked to focus on the lack of gadgets.

"It's really cool," they told their friends. "You have to turn a crank to open the windows."

MAT KNUPP BARTLETT, IL

Rev Your Engines

CARS THAT MADE OUR HEARTS RACE

BURNING SOME RUBBER

In the spring of 1960, I was finishing up my first year at the University of Washington in Seattle. I lived at home but spent many afternoons with my fraternity buddies at the Sigma Phi Epsilon house. One sunny day, as I ate lunch there, I heard the roar of a high-performance car. Within seconds, I was outside.

A sparkling 1959 Polo White Corvette sat in the parking lot. It was surrounded by a dozen Sig Eps. We gazed longingly at the convertible as our friend Alan got out from behind the wheel and basked in all the attention.

When he raised the hood to show off the powerful fuel-injection engine, we practically began to drool. It was beautiful!

"Anyone want a ride?" Alan offered. There were a number of takers, so I eagerly waited for my turn behind the upperclassmen. When I finally buckled in, I said, "Let's burn some rubber."

"That will be easy," Alan said. The Corvette shot down the street like a bullet. In just a few moments, we were around the final turn, coasting back to the house. As I stumbled out of the car, my heart racing, one of my fraternity brothers pointed up the street.

"See those two black streaks? That was you and Alan striping the pavement," he said, pointing at impressive tire tracks that

went north as far as I could see. My '55 Chevy could never burn rubber like that.

From then on, I dreamed about owning a Corvette. My goal was to find an older model for less than two grand.

After months of searching, I caught a break. While getting a haircut, I heard about a 1956 Corvette for sale and decided to give the owner a call. His son had bought the car new and then joined the Marines. Now the dad was selling it.

An hour later, I stopped by to see the car. My first impression wasn't very good. The Corvette had been sitting uncovered for two years and was completely

caked with dust. But underneath the dirt, it was my dream color, Venetian Red.

"If you had come a few days from now, I would've had time to clean it," the seller said. "I'll show you." He grabbed an old towel, wet it and cleaned off the right-front fender. It looked better than I had expected.

After examining the engine and taking a test drive, I offered $1,500, and he accepted. Then the seller pointed out a soft convertible top stored under the hardtop cover. My $1,500 bargain got even sweeter. That's me (above, left) with my mom, my friend John and my long-awaited Corvette.

ED LINCOLN WOODINVILLE, WA

THOUGHT TO REMEMBER ⁓ A little oil may save a great deal of friction.

SUNSET RIDE IN A STING RAY

Uncle Sam planned on drafting me in the late 1960s, so I enlisted in the Army to give myself some choice in duty and training location. My basic training was at Fort Ord on the scenic central California coast.

When it became apparent that I was probably destined for Vietnam, I spent about half of a recent inheritance from my grandmother to buy a 4-year-old 1965 Chevy Corvette Sting Ray (right, at Fort Ord). It was the chance to experience my idea of the ultimate American sports car.

Picking up that bright blue Sting Ray in Monterey was one of the highlights of my life. As the sun started to set over the Pacific Ocean, I headed south from Fort Ord for a short scenic drive toward Big Sur.

As I became comfortable with the Corvette's four-speed transmission and powerful V-8 engine, I punched up a local FM radio station. The song that began to play as I motored along

in near heaven was "Bridge Over Troubled Water" by Simon and Garfunkel. Something in that powerful song spoke to me and made the experience perfect.

To this day, I still own a metallic blue 1960s Corvette Sting Ray,

lovingly maintained for fun road trips, including old Route 66. Having survived those troubled waters of my Army life, I still cherish the memories that flood over me when I hear my song.
JAMES R. DATSKO ELK RAPIDS, MI

CHARIOT OF ICE "My father (behind the wheel, above) and an uncle built this racer around 1922 in my father's auto repair shop in Duluth, Minnesota," says Homer J. Blaisdell, Placentia, California. "The 'Essex' represents the make of the engine, which they rebuilt for racing. Before the racer was finished, my father chose the ice on Lake Superior as the testing ground. They had not completely secured the battery for the test run, so my father sat on the unfinished tail of the car behind the driver and held it in place while they traveled at an estimated 80 to 90 mph. That wide-open ride on the ice must have been a thrill!"

ONE SPEEDY T "This photo was in the Winona, Minnesota, senior high school yearbook in 1938," Gerald Wernecke (behind the wheel) writes from Portland, Oregon. "I bought the Model T, which was a 1922 or '23, from my brother for $10. I entered it in a 100-mile stock car race at the Galesville, Wisconsin, fairgrounds in 1938 or 1939. The race was 200 laps, but I pulled out after 124. After the race, my cousin and I took a 400-mile vacation in that sturdy Model T. I loved that car. It gave me many fond memories."

Road Trip!

HAVE CAR, WILL TRAVEL

SLIPPING THROUGH THE SANDS

My father thoroughly believed in long vacations. Time off always meant going somewhere. In the summer of 1963, we drove our AMC Rambler from Maine to California. We would be gone for a month and intended to see as much of the country as possible.

We took great care in crafting the itinerary. Most of the stops were designed to entertain my mother and me, but Daddy's one must-see was the Bonneville Salt Flats in Utah.

A DASH OF SALT Racers try to set speed records at the famed Bonneville Salt Flats in Utah, where Ellen and her parents (right) stopped on their way to California.

For a hundred years, racers have tested the limits of their vehicles on this smooth, flat surface that by summer's end is as hard as concrete and ideal for racing. In 1914, Teddy Tezlaff was one of the first to set a land speed record here, recording 141.73 mph in a Blitzen Benz.

The flats are in the Great Salt Lake basin, and that part of Utah is hot—but in summer 1963, it was even hotter than usual. The sweltering weather overwhelmed us long before we reached the famous testing grounds.

When we arrived, Daddy wanted a picture of Mama standing in the vastness of the testing grounds. He told her to walk onto the salt flats so he could get the photo without the line of fencing behind her.

When Mama hesitated, he assured her, saying, "It's fine. They race cars on this stuff."

Less than 50 feet off the road, the salt crust did the inevitable and gave way. Mama's face said *I told you so!* better than words as she sank up to her knees in some of the vilest mud on earth.

I screamed that Mama was going under, and Daddy could only dance back and forth in indecision.

After an epic struggle, Mama extricated herself and lumbered to the car, wearing a noxious black substance that was already hardening into a white crust. After a long, smelly and very silent ride, we stopped at a gas station, where the attendant hosed Mama off, snickering the whole time.

ELLEN EVANS WHITING PRINCETON, NJ

CHILLY SIGHTSEEING Kathryn Hart of Downingtown, Pennsylvania, drove this 1956 Oldsmobile from Philadelphia to Anchorage, Alaska. She's seen in '56 with her husband on the Seward Highway near Anchorage, a 127-mile stretch offering vistas of snowcapped mountains and ice blue glaciers.

CORVETTE ADVENTURE "On our honeymoon in November 1971, my wife, Margaret, and I were just 70 miles short of our destination, Minneapolis, when the valve rocker arm on our 1965 Corvette Roadster broke, leaving us stranded on the highway," writes Don Barbini, Thunder Bay, Ontario. "Fortunately I had a tool kit, so I removed the rocker arm and walked to a nearby town to buy a new one. I still have the broken part as a souvenir."

BEWARE THE BACKHOUSE Bruce Thompson, Waukesha, Wisconsin, posed wife Joyce, son Mark and daughter Robin in '75. "I'm pretty sure this is in Wall, South Dakota, a stop on a three-week trip across Canada and back across the northern U.S.," says Bruce. "We camped all the way!"

THOUGHT TO REMEMBER ~ A truly contented person enjoys the scenery along a detour.

ROAD TRIP RESPITE "On our way to Minnesota in 1954, my dad, Jeff Weston, and my sister, Ann, stretched their legs at a gas station," writes Sue O'Neill of Beatrice, Nebraska.

DAD AND HIS JEEPSTER KEPT THEM JUMPING

My younger sister, Janet (left), and I often found ourselves in the backseat of a 1949 Jeepster convertible. Hooked to the rear of the car was a two-wheeled wagon holding all our possessions.

In the summer of 1948, when I was 12, my father decided he didn't like New York state anymore. Our first stop was Munising, Michigan, but after listening to stories about the winters there, he reconsidered and we returned to New York.

The next summer, our family headed to Kennewick, Washington. After two years, we were off again.

We spent a few months in Owosso, Michigan, a few in Albuquerque, New Mexico, and most of my junior year of high school in Conway, South Carolina.

After school let out, Janet and I were in that backseat again, heading to Adrian, Michigan. I started my senior year there. By Thanksgiving, we were rolling to Redding, California.

Traveling with my father was a moving experience...literally!

MARY BUSH MILLER ADRIAN, MI

ACROSS THE COUNTRY IN THE TRUSTY WILLYS-KNIGHT

In 1927, this Willys-Knight four-door sedan safely transported my father, Edward Toperzer, and his two brothers, Curtis and Walter, to California and back to their starting point of Homestead, Pennsylvania. My Uncle Curt was the photographer for the bunch, and years ago, he passed on to me a whole stack of negatives of the places and things they'd seen.

I'm amazed to contrast their driving conditions with everything we have today. If we didn't have to put gasoline in the car or go to sleep or use a restroom, we could drive forever. I remember my dad saying that in those days, roads really didn't exist; they were just dirt and mud, and the wet mud was hard for tires to negotiate. Gas stations were few and far between. There were telephone poles every so often with an old tire nailed to the top, and you drove from one pole to the next. That's how you found your way to wherever you were going. Can you imagine?

Pictured above (from left): Uncle Walt and Dad ham it up, pretending to pull a bolt from a tire; the trio, in heavy coats, are set to board their fully loaded auto; at day's end, the brothers pitch a tent behind their sedan.

EDWARD S. TOPERZER DELTONA, FL

ROCK-SOLID FRIENDS

"Those are my high school pals Gerald Striegel and Bill Woepse in the spring of 1947 at Standing Rock in the Wisconsin Dells," says Jerome Heisdorf of Elkhart Lake, Wisconsin, who took the slide. "I had just received my driver's license and, after a lot of pleading, persuaded my father to let me take my friends in his 1940 Plymouth for the 100-mile drive to the Dells from our home in Sheboygan. We had a most enjoyable day."

THOUGHT TO REMEMBER ~ Let your mind wander, but be careful when you follow it.

▲ BIG TREE MEMORIES

"The highlight of our trip to Yosemite National Park in 1935, when I was 7, was the drive through the giant sequoia known as the Wawona Tunnel Tree," writes Roy Nichols Jr., Reno, Nevada. "My father took this photo (above, left) of my mother and me in our Plymouth. In 1951, while on our honeymoon, my wife, Jane, and I had a picture taken in our Dodge (above, right) at the same tree for a souvenir. Over 2,000 years old, the tree finally fell in 1969 during a heavy snow, closing the road all winter."

◀ WORN OUT AND THIRSTY

"During a family road trip that included a visit to the Seattle World's Fair in 1962, my grandparents' dog Duchess and I stopped at a fountain for a break," says Sandra L. Hicks, Sartell, Minnesota. "A blocked drain had caused the water to pool, so I invited my furry friend up to drink with me. My mother—our trip photographer—thought we looked so cute that she snapped our picture, an all-time favorite of mine."

▼ EARLY FOUR-WHEELIN'

"In 1916, when I was 4, the rural roads we traveled on a family trip had no pavement or bridges, so we drove right through streams in Dad's new Ford Model T Roadster," says Frederick Schuler from St. Petersburg, Florida. "Note we had four spare tires and a spotlight to compensate for the Ford's then very poor headlights."

A PEEK UNDER THE HOOD "My dad, Bill, ran this Shell gas station in Portland, Oregon," writes Tom Chaplin of Moses Lake, Washington. "That's him under the hood of a Cadillac ambulance about 1953, two years before I was born. After talking with my mom, Peggy Stray, and my sister, Carole Start, I learned that the station was only a few blocks from where my parents lived in an apartment."

CHEMICAL REACTION "George and I met in the chemistry lab of a manufacturing company," says Madeline Dent Huss of Bowie, Maryland. "The chemistry between us took, and we were married on Aug. 30, 1952. He was stationed at an Air Force base in Newfoundland but he was able to get back to Lyndhurst, New Jersey, a few days before the wedding."

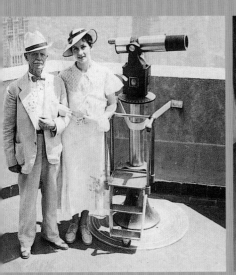

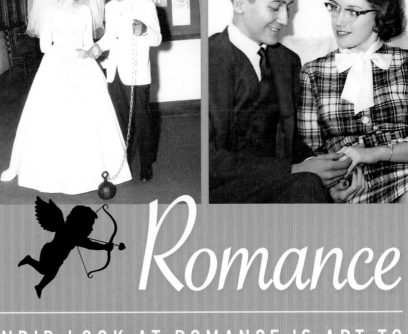

CHAPTER 3

Romance

A CANDID LOOK AT ROMANCE IS APT TO
MAKE ANY HEART SKIP A BEAT. FROM THAT
MEMORABLE FIRST DATE TO THE WEDDING DAY
AND THE BLISS OF MR. AND MRS., IT'S
LOVE AT FIRST SIGHT

How We Met
CUPID'S ARROW HIT THE BULL'S-EYE

LOVE FLOURISHED AT THE FAIR

Home from college in the summer of 1965, I was lucky to be hired as a hostess at the New York World's Fair. For two months, I greeted visitors in the New York State Pavilion—and loved every minute of it.

Guests could ride glass elevators up to three air-conditioned observation towers, where they cooled off and rested their weary feet while taking in a spectacular view. I served them cold drinks and spent time chatting and pointing out different exhibits below.

Shortly after I started, I met a young man named John who also worked at my pavilion as a guide. We became fast friends, spending meal breaks together and visiting other pavilions and exhibits. There was so much to see!

The exhibits from other states and foreign countries seemed endless. The Vatican even displayed Michelangelo's famous Pietà sculpture. When Pope Paul VI visited the fair, John and I spotted him.

What an extraordinary moment.

Because many other fair guides were college students, too, there were lots of chances to socialize. Sometimes, it felt as if I was getting paid to attend an all-day party. Naturally, there were a few jokesters among us. And John became the unsuspecting target of a memorable prank.

One of the elevator operators told his passengers to look for the man standing outside the elevator doors, because his wife had just had a baby. When the doors opened, everyone congratulated John on becoming a new father!

The fair closed in October 1965, and many of us returned for that final weekend. It was sad to say goodbye to so many friends and good times. But for John and me, the adventure had just begun: We got married two years later. Now—two children and five grandchildren later—we continue the journey that began that wonderful summer.

KATHLEEN HOGAN WILMINGTON, DE

COLLEGE STUDENTS
Kathleen and John (right) worked as guides at the 1965 New York World's Fair and started a world-class relationship (above).

SMITTEN Love had just begun to blossom for Mary and Gavin when this photograph was taken in 1956. They married in 1957.

"MAKE ME HAPPY"

It was spring 1956, and I was at a party for the Dolphins girls basketball team. Sponsored by a Catholic Youth Organization club in Downey, California, they had just won a district championship.

A star of the CYO team, Mary Sebastian, was also one of the prettiest girls there. I was enjoying the party, but something was on my mind. I wanted to dance with Mary but hadn't gotten up the nerve to ask her.

I wandered over to the couch where Mary was sitting and began talking and joking with her. Somehow the subject came around to my being single.

"I'm never going to get married," I said. "I'm happy the way I am."

"I don't think you are happy and contented the way you are," Mary replied.

"Well, dance with me, and make me happy."

Mary had a smart retort, but to my surprise, she stood up and accepted my challenge.

Then, for the first time, I held in my arms the girl who would become my wife.

GAVIN CALLINAN WHITTIER, CA

MISSION ACCOMPLISHED "When I began my career as a medical missionary in Pakistan in 1957, matrimony was the furthest thing from my mind...until I met another single missionary, Tom Wiley," says Tilli Wiley of Oley, Pennsylvania. "We married the next year on a friend's porch in 110-degree heat in formal Pakistani clothes: a wool coat for Tom and a white sari for me. Our three children were born in Pakistan, a land we still hold dear after many years of marriage."

MARRIAGE MADE IN THE REED SECTION

Oak Ridge, Tennessee, the home of Oak Ridge National Laboratory, was a small town where all the single people knew one another. Naturally, I was intrigued when a new girl rushed into a seminar I was attending in 1956.

Fortunately, her picture appeared in the next issue of *Lab News*. She was Janet Mitchell, 22, a recent graduate of the University of California.

In my teen years, I had worked as a process server and had learned to track people down. So I managed to find Janet's telephone number. To my surprise, she said yes to a blind date—dinner and a concert.

As we listened to the music, I sensed that Janet had played an instrument before. When she confirmed she'd played saxophone and clarinet, I asked if she'd like to learn the bassoon.

Luckily, our local symphony owned one, and before long, we were playing together in the orchestra and dating (above).

I always made a special effort to play well to impress her, and we've made beautiful music together ever since.

HAROLD KOHN COLUMBUS, OH

THOUGHT TO REMEMBER ➤ The world is full of beauty when the heart is full of love.

MOUSETRAPPED HIM

Back in 1944, a friend on a scavenger hunt came to my apartment looking for a mousetrap. Not finding one, I suggested we check with the friendly couple next door.

Forgetting to knock, I burst in and found them at dinner with two young men. Was my face red!

A few days later, one of the dinner guests called me for a date. Donald and I were married in less than a year.

SHIRLEY CORSE SCARBOROUGH, ME

REPAYING THE DEBT

The ticket seller at a hometown football game shortchanged me 50 cents. I brought it to his attention, but he denied it.

The next day, on lunch break from my bank job, I ran into him. When I mentioned the money he owed me, he said, "I'll take you to the movies instead."

Many times after we were married in 1950, Arthur would kid, "If I give you the 50 cents, can we forget the whole thing?"

MARIANNE PRICE TRUNDY
NEW BEDFORD, MA

NOT JUST A FASTBALL FLING

Jack first caught my eye at a minor league ballgame in 1949. He was a batboy for the Binghamton Triplets in upstate New York, and I thought he was so cute. Just 16, I was very shy and didn't approach him, but that wasn't the last time I saw him.

A few years later, Jack spotted me walking out of a convenience store in my neighborhood. He had to track down "the cute girl in the short shorts" to ask her out, so he called a friend who lived nearby and described me to her. "That's gotta be Jo Young," she said.

Jack was so handsome, he reminded me of Rock Hudson or Cary Grant, but I thought he was conceited because he brought his school baseball album with him on our first date. He called me "spook" because I acted so shy.

He didn't call me again until a year later. It was 1954; he was returning from Army duty with some married friends and needed a date. I agreed, and we went to a local football game. Just a month later, he proposed and we married the next summer. Talk about a whirlwind!

JO HOPPES APALACHIN, NY

ONE FANTASTIC FIND ➤

"I was heartbroken when my boyfriend, Tom, sent me a 'Dear Jane' letter from his Air Force base in Texas telling me he'd met another gal," says Pat O'Barski of Green Valley, Arizona. "A fellow airman named Richard spotted him throwing my photos into a wastebasket and asked Tom for my address. After months of letters and phone calls, Richard visited me in New Jersey, and we agreed to drive to Chicago so I could meet his parents. During my turn at the wheel, I was pulled over for speeding, resulting in a whopping $10 fine. Richard and I married in 1955, and he drove us nearly everywhere."

◄ OUTFIELDER WAS A REAL CATCH

For Peggy Hoehn of Fair Oaks, California, the summer of 1957 was a winning season. A girlfriend introduced her to the outfielder for her local minor league baseball team, the Tri-City Braves. "One word instantly came to my mind: Wow!" she says. "The attraction was mutual. Bob and I got married the following August. I tell our three children and six grandchildren that the baseball diamond produced a true gem!"

▲ TOKEN OF AFFECTION

His pinpoint throw at a boardwalk game booth won Louis Alt a stuffed animal and his longtime crush Barbara's heart. "I'd practiced suave pick-up lines, but instead, I thrust the prize into her arms and stammered, 'Th-this is for you!'" he says from Union, New Jersey. Wed in 1970, they still make an annual anniversary trip back to the boardwalk.

◄ A COUPLE OF DREAMBOATS

"At a party in 1965, an interesting guy named Larry told my friend Nancy and me that he had built a boat and was taking it on its maiden voyage the following day," says Carol Sikorski of Fair Haven, Michigan. "We 'happened' to be at the canal just as he and his cousin Dan were about to launch. Seeing us, they stopped the boat to talk, and we ended up on a double date at a drive-in movie that evening." For Dan and Carol (left) and Larry and Nancy (inset), it's been a *bon voyage* ever since.

Young Love

COLLEGE SWEETHEARTS

On a Friday evening in May 1958, I met a tall, handsome ticket taker at the Starlight drive-in theater in Tyler, Texas. I'd had plans to meet some of my classmates at the drive-in, but my parents insisted I go with them instead. I was rather disappointed, so the attention the ticket taker was giving me that night went unnoticed.

Later, I found out that Adell, the ticket taker, spent the rest of the summer finding out who I was and where I lived. When he called me, I asked how he'd gotten my telephone number. He told me it wasn't easy— he'd paid someone $5 for it! I was impressed.

As luck would have it, Adell attended Texas College, where I'd be starting in fall. When I arrived there as a freshman, I found out he was a football star and very popular on the campus. I felt very flattered by his interest in me—and it never let up.

Adell continued pursuing me, and I continued playing hard to get. We had a typical campus relationship, dating and attending school events together. We talked about getting married, but I was hesitant.

After finishing school, Adell moved to California. Over the summer, I missed him and realized how important he was to me. I joined him in California, where we were married in 1961.

At the height of the civil rights struggle, Adell and I returned to the South to raise our kids, a decision we never regretted. We are both retired from jobs in academia now and are happy great-grandparents.
JERI CADDELL MILLS NACOGDOCHES, TX

MADE FOR EACH OTHER
Jeri and Adell were as in love in 2011 (left) as they were in 1960, when Jeri was crowned queen of Kappa Alpha Psi (above).

THOUGHT TO REMEMBER — The heart that loves is always young.

THE WRITE ONE Letters between Airman Ray E. Cartier and his girlfriend, Karen, pushed the envelope when it came to creativity. They sent heartfelt messages on movie posters, soda straws, a roll of film (above, center) and even confetti. "It took me an hour and a half to read one she sent on a 30-foot roll of Teletype paper (above, left)," says Ray. The passionate pen pals from Arlington, Texas, were engaged on Thanksgiving 1962.

GIRL'S INTUITION Her mom was skeptical when 9-year-old Loretta Williams announced she'd found her future husband. "His name was Don, and he played cops and robbers with my brothers," she writes from Bellefontaine, Ohio. "Seven years later, in 1954, Don and I walked 20 blocks in zero-degree weather and were married before a judge."

FIELD OF DREAMS "When I finished Army basic training in 1951, I returned to my hometown of Coalinga, California, to spend some time with my parents and my fiancee, Barbara McDonald," writes Don Cain of Rochester, Minnesota. "The weather that spring brought out the beauty of the arid land on the west side of the San Joaquin Valley. This picture shows Barbara, now my wife of many years, in a field of poppies and lupines."

INCHY PINCHY "My future wife, Jeannette, was pinching my chin in a parlor game played at a spring 1947 party when we were students at the Oberlin (Ohio) School of Commerce," says Mel Schaefer of Willoughby Hills. "I, in turn, would pinch my hidden lipstick on the chin of the man to my left. Note that he had a smear on his right cheek. He thought the joke was on the guy across the table, another unsuspecting victim. By the time the ploy unfolded, both men's faces were covered with lipstick. Happily retired now, my wife and I still play 'inchy pinchy.'"

IN LINE FOR LOVE Eager to get his driver's license in 1961, George King of Orem, Utah, was irked to find six girls ahead of him at the courthouse window—until he locked eyes with the prettiest one. "Sharon walked to the back of the line, and we started talking," he says. "I'd never felt so glad to be alive. After I flunked the eye test (I'd forgotten my glasses), I found Sharon waiting for me. She gave me her address. We were practically neighbors!" Seven years later, they went back to the courthouse together to get another license just before their August wedding.

SHE NOT JANE "My future parents were at Myrtle Beach, South Carolina, in the summer of 1952 when my momma, Catherine, found this magazine on the sand," writes Rachel Walker of Rock Hill. "I guess they were sweethearts then because they were married a year later. Momma always called Daddy, Charles Long, 'Tarzan' because he had a nice build. It only makes sense that my siblings called me 'Monkey.'"

Wedding Pranks

It's seldom that any wedding comes off without a hitch—especially with friends, relatives and good-humored brides and grooms itching to add even more fun to the joyous occasion.

▲ ALWAYS A BRIDESMAID...

When Jim and Marian Thompson were married in Cleveland, Ohio, in 1953, they had a normal picture taken (small photo, at top). Then the groom and his groomsmen turned the tables on the photographer and posed with the bride's and her attendants' veils and bouquets (above). That's Jim, as the blushing "bride," third from the right.

▲ WEIGHTY COMMITMENT

Nelson Price was a true prisoner of love thanks to three fun-loving older brothers who handcuffed him to a ball and chain. "Nelson lugged it with him as we left the church and all through the wedding reception," says his wife, Linda, of Glendora, California. "We've kept it all these years as a crazy memento of our special day."

◄ TP FOR TWO

A mess of good-hearted shenanigans kept newlyweds Alice and Bob Dooley (opposite, bottom) laughing in 1967. Not only did buddies toilet paper their car, says Alice, of Woodland Park, Colorado, "but when we got home from our honeymoon, we found our bedroom was filled from floor to ceiling with crumpled newspaper. And the church parking lot sign (left) was wired to our bed!"

PROPERTY
CH USE ONLY

THOUGHT TO REMEMBER ~ Love reduces friction to a fraction.

Tying the Knot

MEMORIES RING WEDDING BELLS

VICTORY FOR ROMANCE

The call I'd been waiting for came in October 1943. It was my fiance, Melvin, phoning from Fort Dix, New Jersey: "We got it—the three-day pass plus my seven days earned. How about Sunday?"

By the time he stepped off the troop train at Columbus' Union Station on Saturday, Mother and I had picked up a wedding dress, ordered the cake, alerted the attendants and reserved the church. After a quick hug, Melvin hurried to Fort Hayes for his blood test. But by the time he got his results, the courthouse was closed. We couldn't get the marriage license!

There was one ace in the hole left. We called the judge at home and explained. We were surprised when he answered, "I have a wartime situation here," and instructed us to meet him at the courthouse the next morning.

Two other couples who shared our predicament were there, too. And we all had beautiful weddings, thanks to a judge with real romance in his soul.

MINNIE SHAVER COLUMBUS, OH

"I DO'S" DECLARED

Bill McElwee and his bride, Aloma, sped off in a sporty '58 Corvette in 1966 (above). Groom Bob Mathers (far left with his best man and the pastor) lost the marriage license after admiring it for this 1960s photo.

DOUBLE EXPOSURES

Fabric was difficult to locate for my June 1947 wedding. It was so soon after World War II that even bridal patterns were few and far between. I don't doubt that many brides at the time wed in gowns made from the same pattern—a long train, long buttoned sleeves and a back buttoned to the waist.

When Mama heard that the John A. Brown Co. department store in Oklahoma City had received a shipment of bridal satin, she bought it all. There was enough white fabric for my gown and several pastel shades for the attendants' dresses. Being an accomplished seamstress, Mama naturally planned to sew my dress and seven others.

Though she bought all the satin, she vetoed chiffon fabric for a negligee!

My wedding gown was truly a labor of love. It required a total of 29 tiny satin-covered buttons and handmade loops—17 for the back closing plus 12 for the sleeves. The 7-foot-plus train was patiently hemmed by hand.

I felt beautiful on the day of my wedding. Even the minister remarked on how I looked. That's why I was so disappointed when the photographer called to tell us that his camera had failed. There were no photos!

Our only alternative was to restage the wedding as best we could, retracing our steps at the church and reception. The florist and bakery provided a bouquet of roses and a tiered cake, but we had no minister or guests present. The flower girls, however, were still available and willing to film. All these years later, the rest of the original service survives only in our memory.

JANET CORWIN TAYLOR TULSA, OK

"During our first kiss as man and wife, Jack and I waited for the recessional music to cue our walk down the aisle. But there was only silence, so we kept kissing, and kissing and kissing. My dad, who never learned to whisper, exploded, 'Is that really necessary?' We're still kissing, with or without music."

MAC RUSH BUFORD, GA

Married Life

IN LOVE FROM THIS DAY FORWARD

NEWLYWEDS ROUGHED IT IN ALASKA

Gladys and I (at Behm Canal, right) started housekeeping in a rustic two-room cabin with no electricity, no running water and no telephone. The exterior walls were stuffed with dried tree moss for insulation, and one interior wall was papered with covers from *The Saturday Evening Post*.

The cabin was on a gold-mining operation (center, right) I worked with my uncle, Bert Lee. It was about 30 miles by water north of Ketchikan, Alaska, on the Cleveland Peninsula at Helm Bay.

Gladys and I met at a Norwegian dance in Ketchikan on July 3, 1938. We were married five months later and moved into the cabin (bottom, right).

Our ramshackle palace had a Yukon stove, which was a rectangular box-shaped affair made of light sheet metal.

The bed was a rickety wooden platform with two legs on one side. The other side was nailed to the wall. The bed's "springs" were a 6-inch layer of pine boughs.

Our meager but very useful possessions were two hunting rifles, a splitting ax, a hotcake griddle, a teakettle and a washtub.

We were surrounded by thick woods with abundant wildlife as our nearest neighbors. There were deer and bears, and on some hushed nights, we could hear the howls of wolves echoing as they made their rounds.

The bald eagle ruled the air, while little furry animals scurried among the trees, rustling through the brush on the forest floor.

Our 15 memorable months at the Blue Jay Mine were a very happy and exciting beginning for our marriage.

LE ROY BELSHEE POULSBO, WA

THOUGHT TO REMEMBER ➤ True love is more than holding hands; it's holding hearts.

SWEETHEART OF A GUY

Mom and Dad were never the demonstrative type. This was especially so in the presence of us kids as we grew up in Jefferson City, Missouri, in the 1950s.

Dad was a blue-collar kind of guy. He worked 8 to 4 and wasn't one for gabbing.

When it came to showing tender feelings, Dad was a shy man. We five kids knew Mom and Dad loved each other, but I can't remember a time when I heard either of them say it.

We loved to walk into the kitchen and catch Mom sitting in Dad's lap. Mom would jump up like a teenager caught smooching with her boyfriend in the front room. One day we really looked forward to was Valentine's Day, when a ritual took place at our house that I remember with great tenderness.

It seems Mom would always be in the kitchen cooking. Dad would pull into the drive and come into the house with a sheepish look on his face. We kids would be watching TV.

He would then walk in, one hand behind his back, and ask in a gruff voice, "Don't you kids have something else to do?"

"No. Why?" was our standard response.

Dad would get red in the face, hem and haw, and then walk past us and into the kitchen.

Behind his back was always a huge, red, heart-shaped box of chocolates. Of course, we acted as though we'd seen nothing. We could hear whispering in the kitchen, then a suspicious silence.

Dad would come back into the living room, looking pleased with himself, and settle into his recliner. Mom would call us into the kitchen to see the beautiful box of candy and allow us each "just one."

The rest of that evening, we'd catch Mom and Dad glancing at each other with knowing looks.

Love isn't always vocal or showy. It is standing together to face the future, relying on each other and teaching your children to respect themselves and others.

And sometimes, it's just a shy, sweet man bringing a box of chocolates to his wife after many years of marriage, five kids and an enduring love.

ELAINE SCHEPERS-THOMPSON
HOLTS SUMMIT, MO

DELICIOUS SECRET The author's dad, Clarence Schepers, tried to be sneaky in his displays of affection for wife Helen. They (at right, and as newlyweds in 1943, inset) didn't need words to express their love.

TOP O' THE WORLD "My parents, Florence and Willis Townsend, visited the Empire State Building on their honeymoon in 1935," writes Angela Townsend, Miami Beach, Florida. "Dad, a widower at 77, and Mom, 27, had four of us in nine years."

DINER ROMANCE "Every morning after his night shift, my dad, John Mullin (seated), ate breakfast at the Rainbow Diner in Chester, Pennsylvania. My mother, Marie (center), was a waitress there for 18 years," says Marie Mullin Jadick of Cape May, New Jersey.

GOOD MORNING, DEER "This picture (below) was snapped in Mesa, Arizona, on Sept. 20, 1928," writes Mesa resident Helen Freeman. "It shows my parents, Albert and NaDene Harper, on their wedding day. The other photo, taken during their honeymoon at Yosemite National Park, is of Mom getting a kiss from a friendly deer."

HAPPY HARMONY "When my parents, Charles and Emily Krcma (far right), celebrated their golden wedding anniversary in 1963, all 13 of us children gathered around Dad's old music box for this photograph," says Marjorie Luckow of Manitowoc, Wisconsin. "We spent many enjoyable hours listening to that music box together."

POST-WAR SMILES "We posed on the steps of the Detroit Yacht Club after our wedding breakfast in 1946," says Elaine Creagh Griffith of Grosse Pointe, Michigan. "It was so special. The guys were back from the war, including two brothers of my husband, Myles. All my sisters served as my bridesmaids."

FRESH FLOWERS
"I couldn't imagine why my flower box geraniums kept vanishing as soon as they bloomed," says Jean Jones of Wilmot, South Dakota. Then she discovered what little sprouts Billy, 2, and Lois Ann, 1, were up to in August of 1957.

CHAPTER 4

Home Sweet Home

HOME ISN'T ONLY WHERE THE HEART IS.
IT'S THE DOORWAY TO COUNTLESS
MEMORIES OF FUN TIMES SPENT WITH
FAMILY AND FRIENDS...AT AN ADDRESS
YOU'LL NEVER FORGET

Our House

IF THESE WALLS COULD TALK

ALL FIRED UP
John and Cecile Brown spend time with nine of their children (at right) in the early 1950s. Below, John has his arms full of twins Mickey and Rickey, toddler Myrtle and baby Mary June, who is also in his hands as the twins play on a truck (opposite page). Fire Station No. 1 is now a tourist information center.

FIRST FAMILY OF OLD NO. 1

When our family moved into the upper floor at Fire Station No. 1—actually, the only one in Plaquemine, Louisiana, in 1941—I was just 2. Back then, there were only my parents, John and Cecile Brown, my big sister, Joan, and me on the scene. The great thing about where we lived was that Dad was a fireman, so he was on the job!

Our home featured a large dormitory-type room across the front, a bedroom backing it, and then a dining area, bath and kitchen joined by a hallway. We entered from a stairway that led up to a second-story porch—alas, no brass pole to slide down.

Dad installed a gate at the top of the stairs and screened in the porch with chicken wire to keep baby bottles from falling to the sidewalk. That was a wise idea: By the time we moved out 15 years later, I had five more sisters and five brothers, requiring us to double and triple up in our beds.

Our school was right across the street from the fire station, so we could come home for lunch. We did homework on the screened porch on nice days or in the hall when the weather was bad. There

was a small yard to play in, or we could go to the school playground. We walked everywhere, because we had no car; I was 14 before Dad bought his truck.

Mom had so much love for all us kids, and I think this kept us from fighting. She volunteered for years as secretary of the firemen's auxiliary. Dad let us climb and play on the fire trucks, but only when he was there to watch us.

Life was fun at our unusual home, although we certainly had outgrown it by 1956, when city officials made plans to demolish the second floor and build a firemen's dormitory in the back. Two more fire stations were planned for Plaquemine at the same time. Not only had our family grown, so had our city.

My parents found a 14-room house to rent for $25 a month just two blocks away from the fire station—and, wow, it had two bathrooms. Almost no waiting!

But I didn't get to enjoy the big house for long. In 1957, I married and got ready to start my own family. Two years later, Mom gave us a baby brother to bring the kid count to a baker's dozen. Today I have six sisters and six brothers, all doing well.

We weren't the first family to live in Plaquemine's Fire Station No. 1, just the largest—and, of course, the last.

BETTY BROWN ROCKFORTE PLAQUEMINE, LA

"In this fun 1960 photograph, our daughter Zona is having a high time at home, playing with her superstrong daddy, Skip Wick."

GINNY WICK HURLEY, WI

▼ PHOTOGRAPHER TOOK HOME TO WORK

"My father, William Alexander, a professional photographer, built this house on wheels on a Ford chassis in 1920 so we could travel on jobs," says Dorothy Canfield, Brewster, Washington (seated left, with mom and siblings in bottom photo). "It had two gas stoves, a kitchen cabinet, lavatory, folding bed and phonograph. We did most of our traveling in Washington, where Dad took pictures of people and wheat harvests. He used a tent as a studio and the tent or the house as a darkroom. During the school year, we lived in a 'stationary' house."

▲ BEDTIME BOPPING

"When I told my kids I was going to take pictures of them pillow fighting, they said, 'Oh, goody!'" says Bob Taylor from Cordell, Oklahoma. "I turned them loose, and they had a big time. Susan was about 6 years old and Gregg was about 4, and he had already started to catch up to her in size. This memorable pillow fight took place in our bedroom in the winter of 1957, when I was running my business Agricultural Photos here in town."

◄ FUNNIES WERE FABULOUS
"We got a Sunday paper only once in a while, so it was a big treat," says Lorita Thornhill of St. Peters, Missouri. "On this Sunday in 1945, my father, Edgar Wussler, my sister, Marilyn, 8, and I, 4, were very intent on reading the paper on our back porch in St. Charles. That's my 2-year-old brother, Donald, looking curiously through the screen door."

▲ LINES OF COMMUNICATION
"Hanging out wash did not have to be drudgery when it was shared with friends in 1958," says Pauline Bowyer, Caledonia, Illinois. "My dad, Tom Gandolfo, took this photo of our neighbor Angela as she and my mother were chatting and hanging clothes from our adjacent apartment buildings in the Bronx, New York. Most women on our block were stay-at-home moms and homemakers."

▲ MR. GABBY "Our first son, Roger, loved to talk on the telephone and use the 'gab stool' that we had back then in our apartment in Harvey, Illinois. He also liked his little pipe," writes Marge Fraser of Lockport. "This slide was taken in 1958 one evening after Roger had taken his bath and was relaxing before going to bed."

THOUGHT TO REMEMBER ▷ Character, like a house's foundation, is below the surface.

On the Farm
WHERE ROOTS GROW DEEP

WHEN TEENS RULED THE FARM

In May 1947, my folks took two of my sisters—Jiggs, 16, and Jeanette, 14—and me, 15, out of school in Milwaukee and put us to work on our family's central Wisconsin farm in Vesper. My parents stayed behind to work in the city.

We'd farmed the land from 1938 to 1942 before moving to Wisconsin Dells and then Milwaukee. We were likely sent back to the farm to keep an eye on the land.

Our farm was the only one on the road, so we had no electricity. Instead we relied on kerosene lamps and lanterns.

There was no phone, either, and we walked more than a mile into town to get our mail. Water came from a well, and we used a pail and rope to bail out enough for our needs. On cold days, the outhouse was a long walk away.

That fall, we went to high school in nearby Rudolph. Jiggs soon went back to school in Milwaukee, leaving Jeanette and me to mind the farm. When the weather got really cold in November, I figured this was no place for my sister. So without telling my mother, I scrounged up $10 and sent Jeanette back home on the train.

Living alone on the farm was an adventure and a test of self-sufficiency, especially when temperatures fell below zero. To stay warm, I would put a blanket over the door to keep the heat in.

A woodstove in the kitchen provided the heat. To feed it, I had to chop up part of the barn. I was so grateful when a farmer came by and sold me a face cord of wood for $3.75; I remember the exact amount because it was all the money I had to my name.

To stay warm at night, I would fill the woodstove, then set my alarm clock for midnight so I could refill the stove. Sometimes, I'd sleep through the alarm and wake up to find no fire burning and my water frozen solid.

Everyone knew I lived alone, and nobody made a fuss about it. It was a different era.

I graduated from high school in 1950 and moved to Milwaukee to work. In the late 1960s, I bought my own farm in Colgate. You can take the kid off the farm, but you can't take the farm out of the kid.

JIM SHORT COLGATE, WI

RESILIENT TEENS Jiggs (from left), Jeanette and Jim Short were sent to tend their family farm in central Wisconsin while their parents remained in the city to work.

THE ICEMEN "CUT-ETH" "This photo of my father, Amos W. Vieira (right), and his brother Fred cutting ice on their farm pond in Jacksonville, Illinois, was taken about 1921," writes Nadine Stewart from Jacksonville. "They stored their ice in sawdust for later use. The family had six boys, but this chore was always assigned to these two."

SOCIAL CLIMB "Taken in 1957, this picture brings back fond memories of apple picking with this ladder," says Dolores Miller from Sheboygan, Wisconsin. "That's my late husband, Jim Miller, with our dog Teddy, who loved to climb the ladder and visit. The tree bears Jonathan apples, and we trucked many bushels of those and other varieties to sell as a sideline to our dairy farming. My son David still runs the Manitowoc County farm that's been in our family for generations."

TATER ANTICIPATORS "My brothers Dean, 11, and Dale, 7, help harvest a bountiful potato crop in the fall of 1953 on the Isaacs family farm near Hazel Run, Minnesota," writes Linda Isaacs of Norman, Oklahoma. "Judging by their grins, they're likely anticipating Mom's delicious scalloped potatoes!"

THOUGHT TO REMEMBER ➤ Sow seeds of kindness and you'll enjoy a perpetual harvest.

▲ **BALES O' FUN** "Our dog, Rex, got atop bales of straw with our children, Gregory, Kevin and Paula, on a chilly day in the early '60s," say Barbara and Walter Mohr of Millington, Michigan. "The slide was taken on the family farm near Otter Lake. That's Grandpa Mohr's 1955 Chevrolet pickup truck."

➤ **AXLE-HIGH CORN** "My parents, Marvin and Doris Hostetler, were married in January 1935," says Jerald Hostetler from Orrville, Ohio. "They took over Dad's family's Sugardale Holstein Farm near Orrville that spring. This slide of Dad was taken in the late 1930s. He's aboard his 1935 Farmall tractor, in the middle of cultivating corn."

◀ MOTHER HEN

"My mother, Mary Bombik, is feeding chickens at her summer home in Auburn Corners, Ohio," writes Josephine Koces of Cleveland. "She stayed there all summer because she loved the quiet country setting." Her home, at far right, was an old voting building the family bought and moved to the 5-acre site.

► THE HOUSE OUT BACK

"There was a well-worn path between our farmhouse and what we called 'going to see Mrs. Jones,'" says David Michaelson, Balsam Lake, Wisconsin. "In winter, there was often a nice white frosty ring around the receptacle. That's probably what our outhouse guest found shortly after I snapped her picture."

▲ STOPPING TO SAY "HAY!"

"My father, Delbert Walker, is taking a break from baling hay to pose with my sister around 1950 at our Hanford, California, farm," says John Walker, who now lives north of there in Clovis. "After serving in the Army Air Corps during World War II, he came home to try his hand at farming."

Family Meals

Remember those melt-in-your-mouth moments? Whether it's Sunday dinner at Grandma's, a backyard picnic or a hands-on baking lesson from Mom, you can practically taste the love.

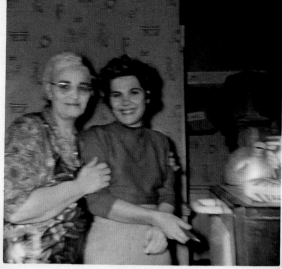

JUN ➤ 60

◄ LAYERED WITH LOVE

"I spent much of my childhood swaddled in an apron helping Mama and Nona (above) prepare Italian feasts," says Rebecca Brothers (left) of Niles, Ohio. "We'd layer pan after pan of lasagna made with garden-fresh tomatoes and garlic and homemade noodles. These days, I continue our family tradition by organizing church dinners for the community."

▲ LASTING FAVORITES

"Here I am with my children and husband in the 1960s," writes Donna Lundy of Zearing, Idaho. "We were photographed for a feature in our local newspaper that included my recipes. I'm still cooking in this same kitchen and still making many of the same family favorites."

SUMMERTIME SNACK

"My brother, Danny Barkley, and I are sharing a watermelon with our aunt Rosie Blizzard on a summer day in 1953 at my grandparents' home in Cates, Indiana," says Sherrie Cheesman, of Terre Haute.

OVEN FRESH "This picture of me and my son, Gary, advertised a local bakery's brown-and-serve rolls and appeared in our newspaper in June 1950," writes Gene Marsh of Knoxville, Tennessee. Gary still has this smile on his face whenever he returns home to enjoy his mother's home cooking.

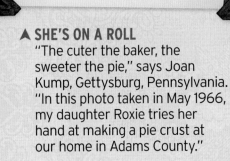

SHE'S ON A ROLL

"The cuter the baker, the sweeter the pie," says Joan Kump, Gettysburg, Pennsylvania. "In this photo taken in May 1966, my daughter Roxie tries her hand at making a pie crust at our home in Adams County."

THOUGHT TO REMEMBER Grandma's cookies didn't need preservatives—they didn't last that long.

Cherished Pets
OUR FURRED AND FEATHERED FRIENDS

ANIMAL ACTIVIST

I grew up with lots of pets around our home in Coleman, Texas, in the 1950s and '60s. My father, Dr. Roy Kemper, kept the town healthy for nearly 30 years. Because of his tender heart, he happily treated plenty of ailing animal patients as well.

We had the usual line of dogs and cats, but we also provided a foster home for all kinds of wild animals. The whole town knew of Dad's willingness to take in almost anything in need of healing. We bottle-fed baby skunks quite often that actually made wonderful pets—some "de-scented" and some not.

My first favorite pet was a gray fox named Reynard that Dad received as a recently born orphan. I would cuddle up and sleep with him in his bed. My brothers had a cage made for rehabilitating large birds—hawks, falcons and owls included. And we sometimes sheltered an injured calf or other livestock while they were on the mend.

Critters appeared in the strangest places. I won't forget finding a whirling dervish in the bathtub. My shriek caught Dad's attention, and he showed me it was a feral cat in need of TLC.

Dad once found a litter of short-haired "Heinz 57"-type pups that looked like border collies. They were really smart, so we gave one that we named Corky to my grandpa to mind his farm, and kept another we called Bubby.

On car trips in Dad's 1960 Chevy, Bubby would climb out the back window when we weren't looking and up onto a fin, walking up the side of the car to watch from out there. I don't know how he kept from falling off! He'd do the exact same thing at the lake, standing on the bow

of the boat with his ears flapping away in the wind.

Most of what I've described may now be illegal, but in that time, it was just natural, at least in our animal-crazy family.

ANITA KEMPER CALK
SILVER VALLEY, TX

A REGULAR MENAGERIE Pets cared for by the author and her father (top right) and their family included (below, from left) Reynard the fox, Corky the farm dog and family cat Kittnen.

GIMME A HUG "As you can tell from this picture, taken in winter 1954 in New Britain, Connecticut, my dog Baron and my cat Bootsey got along well," writes George Scheyd of Newington. "We bought Baron as a purebred German shepherd puppy. Bootsey, a stray cat, jumped into my car one day when I was out shopping; he'd sit on this Casco folding chair and look out the window. Incidentally, many years later, we still use that Casco chair."

"My mother, Jane Wilkinson, taught us a lot about compassion for animals. While growing up in Austin, Texas, we always had pets around—mostly dogs and cats. In this photo from about 1953, you can see how she provided kittens with a safe place to stay!"

TARA HOUGHTON DOROTHY, NJ

FIVE-AND-DIME BIRD "After graduating from high school in 1958, I decided to get my mom a special Christmas gift," says Linda Thompson of Citrus Heights, California. "I found the perfect one at the local five-and-ten store— a feisty green parakeet she named Tweety Bird. His favorite activity, besides cuddling with Mom, was preening in front of the iron (above, left). Mom ironed everything, so Tweety had lots of conversations with his reflection."

THOUGHT TO REMEMBER Birds have bills too, but they keep on singing.

▲ **PRIZEWINNING POOCH** "Our beagle, Pebble, scored this trophy at a field trial in 1957," writes Linda Sprouse-Scott, Midlothian, Virginia. "That's my father, Robert Rash, and my brother Wayne sitting with our proud pup on the porch."

◄ COLLIE CAPTURED THEIR HEARTS

"Years ago, a woman came into our place of business and mentioned she raised collies," says Patricia Crim, Coquille, Oregon. "She said she had a new litter and one pup didn't measure up, so she offered him to my dad. This golden ball of fluff that we named Lance grew rapidly and was well-mannered and loving. The same woman stopped back later and agreed that our Lance had turned out to be the most beautiful of all her collies."

► BEWARE THE DOG

"My dog, Patsy, was very protective of me," Beatrice Lehman Henriott of Knox, Indiana, writes. "If anyone pretended to harm me, Patsy would growl and bare her teeth. She's on 'guard duty' in this 1932 photo."

▲ PETS AT PLAY

"My pony, Rex, and I stopped outside our home near Galena, Kansas, for this 1944 snapshot," writes Jack Dunn from Wichita. "My dad, Perry, and our dog, King, got in on the posing, too."

Around the Yard
FUN IS RIGHT AT YOUR DOORSTEP

DAD'S DIY RINK IS A REAL ICEBREAKER

In the early '60s, our little town of Erie, Pennsylvania, didn't have indoor ice rinks. There were frozen ponds scattered around the countryside, but the one I liked best was in our own yard, built every winter by my dad, Bill. Dad started making his skating rinks as soon as we had the first good freeze. He would fill his lawn roller with steamy hot water and pull it around the yard with his tractor.

The hot water kept the snow from sticking to the roller, and the compacted snow held the water, which was sprayed on after the roller treatment.

Dad was meticulous about the spraying. His secret was to keep the passes of water light and repeat the spraying every hour. It took three or four days, but the result was a smooth, glistening rink that attracted people from all over the county.

Dad let everyone skate for free. He even kept extra skates hanging in the basement, available on a "help-yourself" basis. Mom usually provided hot chocolate and coffee. We had a wood-burning stove to keep us warm, and a plank on two crates made a serviceable bench.

The final touch was music—from waltzes to The Beatles on the record player or from my oldest sister, Sandy, on her accordion. Mom threw a fit when Dad drilled through the living room wall to wire an outdoor speaker. But once the music started, she settled down.

When the highway department cleared our road, the plows would send up a salty slush, some of which fell on Dad's pristine ice. He quickly let his displeasure be known, and the plows slowed down when they came past "Maki's rink."

Dad became a skating instructor, too, thanks to a book, *Championship Skating* by Gustav Lussi. It taught such things as figure eights and sit spins.

This all helped my sister Cindy and me become pretty decent skaters. We weren't of Olympic caliber, but when Erie's first winter carnival was held in 1963, we won some nice prizes in the Silver Skates Derby.

And we owed it all to that great "iceman," our dad.

JOHN MAKI ERIE, PA

SLICK TRADITION The author (in striped sweater) poses with his family on the backyard ice rink created by his father, Bill Maki (gliding at right).

THE BIGGEST SNOWBALL EVER

"It took six of us—my sisters (Fran and Jay), my husband (Eddie), my brother-in-law (Ossie), Dad and me—to roll this monster-size snowball back in 1939," writes Ann Simonini, Darien, Illinois. "You needed a lot of open space to roll a snowball of this size. It measured 5 feet in diameter!"

FrAN   JAY   Eddie ossie DAd

ABSOLUTELY ABOMINABLE

Believe it or not, the Abominable Snowman visited the sleepy town of Acushnet, Massachusetts, where I grew up, not once but three times.

The first was during the winter of 1966, an event captured in this photo (left). I'm the little one dressed in red. My aunt Germaine Stephens is the teenager behind me, with my sister Jo Ann Costa Deslauriers between us. My brothers Danny (back) and Marc are standing on the other side.

Our father, Daniel, built the snowman in our backyard, using his Marine Corps sword to carve its features.

The snow creature returned in 1969 and made its final appearance after the blizzard of 1978. It seems as if snow was much deeper back then. I now live with my husband and two sons in a place where the snowman never visits.

LISA COSTA OELLERICH
AUGUSTA, GA

THOUGHT TO REMEMBER → No snowflake in an avalanche ever feels responsible.

▲ OFF TO THE RACES! "I was about 3 years old in 1961 when this photo was taken by my mother," says Kim Summers of Scottsdale, Arizona. "I had accepted the challenge from my dad, Ken Koplitz, to race to the finish line on our newly poured driveway in Everett, Washington. I don't remember if I won the race, but I had a grand time trying!"

◄ ALL SMILES "My Aunt Mabel let loose with her mom, Carrie, on a spring day around 1956," says Thomas W. Metz of Allentown, Pennsylvania. "Mabel (right) looked like a tough woman, but she had a really powerful sense of humor."

"Trying to survive an Arizona summer in the early 1960s, our young family made do with a stainless steel cattle tank and a kiddie pool when temperatures topped 100 degrees. It wasn't the most elegant arrangement, but we certainly enjoyed it!"

JAMES G. LLOYD MESA, AZ

THOUGHT TO REMEMBER ➤ If the grass looks greener on the other side of the fence...fertilize.

"HMM...NOW WHERE IS THAT LEFTOVER ROAST?" "Our family has always enjoyed this picture of Dottie, taken around 1956 by my first husband, Paul Lindstrom," writes Florie Morrison, Arlington Heights, Illinois. "Dottie came into his childhood home as a puppy and brought so much happiness with her. Paul, a camera buff, developed this photo in his basement darkroom. He really captured Dottie's personality."

READY, SET, GO! "Soap Box Derbies were the drag races of the 1940s, without the powerful engines, of course," writes George Robertson of Dyersburg, Tennessee. "At the bottom of the wooden ramp, there was a little bump that launched some of us into the air, but we were still able to stay in our lanes. The kids in this photo—including me, No. 7—are now in our 70s."

CHAPTER 5

Fun & Games

IT'S REALLY NOT WHETHER YOU WIN
OR LOSE. WHEN IT COMES TO SPORTS,
HOBBIES AND JUST-FOR-LAUGHS PASTIMES,
IT'S HOW MUCH FUN YOU HAVE WHILE
YOU'RE AT IT

Go Team!

HEY, NOW THAT'S THE SPIRIT

HIGH HOPES AND LOTS OF HEART

I was crushed when I didn't get accepted onto the cheerleading squad in my freshman year of high school. Becoming a cheerleader at Staten Island's Curtis High School, one of the biggest and best high schools in New York City, was quite an honor.

I always sensed my height held me back. At 5 foot 10, I towered over the other girls. Still, I could perform any feat my more petite counterparts did. I practiced all the following year in the privacy of my bedroom, perfecting cheers I already knew.

In tryouts the second year, my jumps were high, my arm movements precise and my cartwheels straight. To my knowledge, my school was the only one whose cheerleaders performed cartwheels in 1960.

On the last day of tryouts, we gathered anxiously for the reading of names. When mine was called, I leaped forward, nearly knocking over the newly formed lineup, which included my friend Carolyn Mitchell. (I'm at far right and Carolyn's fourth from right in the above photo; that's me with Carolyn, in pink, at right in 2005.) We all cried and hugged and set our sights on the city championships.

Despite bruised knees and aching muscles from months of daily practice, we dry-cleaned our burgundy and white corduroy uniforms and polished our brown and white saddle shoes.

Everywhere we went, we'd sing "Heart" from the musical *Damn Yankees*. That would be our theme song, leading up to our grand entry into the college gym on the day of the big cheer tournament.

The first team performed a flawless routine. Seeing our downcast faces, the captain

gathered us in a huddle before we took the floor.

"You've gotta have heart," she began to sing softly. That did it! Grinning from ear to ear, we began our cheers and launched into a near-perfect performance that ended with our well-choreographed cartwheels.

The amazed crowd gasped at the fan of legs unfolding. Then came thunderous applause.

I held my breath as the announcer named the third- and second-place winners, and then called out, "First place goes to…the Curtis High School cheerleading squad!"

We tumbled and stumbled out of the stands, racing to accept our trophy and individual gold megaphones.

We proved that we had heart.
SUZANNE BEYERS BOTHELL, WA

FUN WAS THEIR GOAL

Back in the '30s, the members of the Merrymount Blackhawks found a slick way to make our own entertainment.

We skated on this pond just off Moffet Road in the Merrymount section of Quincy, Massachusetts.

We had skates, sticks and a borrowed puck. The team uniform was our white caps. There were no coaches and no referees… just fun with our brothers and neighbors. (I'm seated in the middle, at right, and my brother, Gus, is at far right in back.)

I remember one game when we were ahead 16-0. That meant the mascot, me, got in the game as goalie. The other team got off a shot. I put down my stick, but the puck hit a piece of snow or a rut in the ice and jumped over my stick for a goal. My days as a player were over.

BOB EDDY ALTON, NH

MAJOR THRILL FOR MAJORETTE

I had just been named the head drum majorette of the Theodore Roosevelt Junior High School band in San Jose, when our director, Albert Taix, was asked if the band would march at the 1939 Golden Gate International Exposition in San Francisco.

I had so admired the previous majorette, Dorothy Taylor, and hoped that one day I would wear the tall furry hat. I practiced twirling and throwing my baton for hours on end and finally reached my dream.

My dad was so proud to see this picture in the *San Jose Mercury Herald* that he hurried down to the newspaper office and asked for the shiny negative. I rediscovered it while clearing out old scrapbooks, and I've had the photo among my childhood treasures ever since.

BARBARA BONE CORRIN
PLEASANTON, CA

THOUGHT TO REMEMBER ▸ Teamwork divides the effort and multiplies the effect.

◄ **LOCKER ROOM BALLYHOO**

"We Bulldogs from Dugger, Indiana, were a happy bunch in 1949 after our football team defeated Clinton, our archrival," says Richard Hiatt, Atkinson, Illinois. "Our team went on to win eight games with only one defeat. I am on the far right, in front with the striped T-shirt, and my brother Don is next to me with his hand on my shoulder. Our dad is behind me with the cap. He attended all our games to make sure we did our very best."

▲ **READY TO HOOP IT UP**

"My grandmother Dorothy Hawk Hodgson (sitting at right of basketball) played guard for the Rose Hill High School basketball team in Rose Hill, Iowa—even though she was only 5 feet tall," writes Deborah Stiner of Geneseo, Illinois. "The photo was taken in 1932. Note that the very proper players are wearing nylons with their uniforms!"

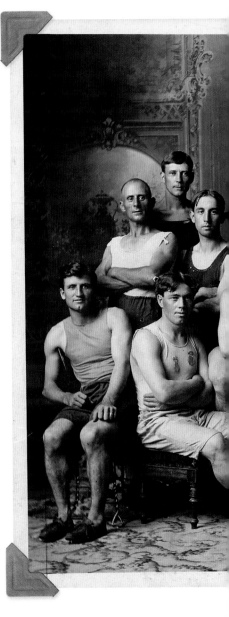

▲ THE LITTLE TEAM THAT COULD

"I'm the small guy at far left in the back on the 1945 Midgets football team of Christian Brothers Academy, a college-prep school in Albany, New York," writes Wally Malek of Defreestville. "It was my first year there. Coached by Brother Roberts, we were quite different from today's tall, brawny players. I wonder what their secret is!"

▲ PLAY BALL

"As a military family, we moved a lot, so I played only one year of Little League, 1956," writes David Kier of Aptos, California. "The highlight of that wonderful summer was the only home run I've ever hit. I was tripped by one of my own teammates as I crossed home plate. As I dusted myself off, I heard laughter, but I didn't care. I had my homer!"

◄ BLAZING FAST SPEED

With spiked shoes and muscular features, the 1901 competitive fire-wagon-pulling team from Marshalltown, Iowa, set a time record that went unbroken for 20 years. "My husband's grandfather and great-uncle were members," says Loraine Buchwald of Oklahoma City, Oklahoma. The family legacy continued with her father-in-law and grandson both serving as firefighters.

Join the Club

One of the best ways to become well-rounded is joining a social circle. Usually, your club membership card guarantees new friendships and memories that will last a lifetime.

BADGE OF HONOR Young Grace Bornschein (above) took part in the Girl Scout's first cookie sale. Her daughter (above, right) later carried on the tasty tradition.

MAKING COOKIE "DOUGH"

In 1933, at age 11, I was a Girl Scout in Erie, Pennsylvania, and had the privilege of participating in the very first year of the national Girl Scout cookie sale.

The price at that time was 15 cents for 12 sugar cookies—the only flavor. This was during the Great Depression, and 15 cents was quite a sum. To advertise the sale, a promotional picture was taken of me selling cookies to a neighbor.

In 1955, our family moved to Louisville, Kentucky, and I had a little Girl Scout of my own, my daughter, Joyce. I continued to work as a Scout leader. At a council meeting in 1958, I mentioned that I had been part of the first sale and had a picture of myself selling cookies. The other members asked if they could use it. They then took a picture of my daughter selling cookies and sent both photos to the *Louisville Courier-Journal*, which ran them along with a story at cookie sale time.

Years later, in March 2008, I was watching the news, and there was a segment on the Girl Scout cookie sale. To my surprise, my 1933 picture popped up on the screen. That evening, my daughter and son called to say they'd seen me delivering my cookie pitch on national TV.

GRACE BORNSCHEIN LOUISVILLE, KY

CARDS, CONVERSATION AND COFFEE

During the 1950s, my mom, Mildred Courtney (second from right), and five neighborhood ladies would get together once a month to socialize, gossip and play cards. At that time, my parents lived in Ferguson, a suburb of St. Louis. The women were a close-knit little community, but as the years passed, most of them moved away, including my mother. This left them with many pleasant reminiscences, for sure. The three women on the left are (left to right) Bobbie Brunk, Rose Pilla and Mary Geislinger. On the far right is Mrs. Hagenhoff, and on the opposite side of my mom is a woman I can't identify.

ROGER COURTNEY FLORISSANT, MO

GROOVY GIRLS CLUB

By the time we hit high school, in 1965, girls clubs whose uniforms had matching satin jackets, as immortalized in the movie *Grease*, were passé. In our club, we wore groovy matching yellow sweatshirts with our club name, "Shawntays," emblazoned in orange on the back.

We formed our own girls social club at Verdugo Hills High School in Sunland-Tujunga, California. The word Shawntay was an attempt by 15-year-old girls to sound both elegant and groovy at the same time. *Enchanté* was the root word (blame freshman French class). It made each girl "a Shawntay," or enchanted.

At first, other clubs laughed at our club because we were all freshmen. That quickly changed when we started throwing the best dances with the best bands—including the Strawberry Alarm Clock. We rocked!

Top-secret criteria for being popular in the 1960s included: 1. Boys have to like you, but you have to have a good reputation. 2. Get passing grades, but don't be an egghead. 3. Own a "boss" car, or have a cute boyfriend with one. 4. Have long, straight hair like Cher or a bubble hairdo like Sandra Dee. 5. Dance as well as Goldie Hawn. 6. Attend senior prom with your senior boyfriend, or have a cute boyfriend in college.

We did some charity work, holding fund-raising dances for worthy causes. But mostly, our club money went toward renting a place at the beach for Easter week. One poor mother would chaperone 15 teenage girls, but we'd meet lots of boys.

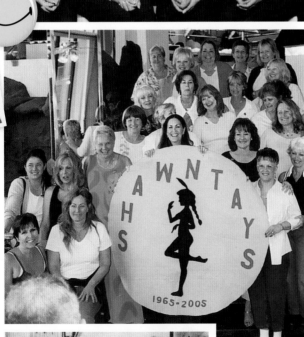

HIP, FUN, MOD
That's how author Linda Peters-Yuro describes the qualities of a Shawntay. The girls club historian, Linda (in top snap, and at right, in middle of back row at a 2005 reunion) remains good friends with many members, whom she credits with building her self-confidence.

The ultimate trip was to Bob's Big Boy in Van Nuys on Wednesday night (club night). Cars full of teens from all over Southern California would be backed up for miles.

For me, the friends I made in high school know who I really am. I can't put on airs because they call me on it. They keep me real.

LINDA PETERS-YURO OXNARD, CA

WHOA, NELLIE! HE WAS JAMMIN' IN THE ROLLER DERBY

I really had the bug to skate on the banked track they used in the Roller Derby. Back in the Derby's golden years in the '50s, it was on television 50 times a year and watched by more fans than football or basketball.

In 1950, I was 15 and living with my Russian emigrant parents in Los Angeles. I was a skater and captain of the Westchester Skateland's speed skating and roller hockey teams.

It was a Friday night in July when Bert Wall and Sid Harnesk, the Chicago Westerners' legendary coach and captain, asked me to try out for the Roller Derby. There were problems, though. I was only 15, and you had to be 18 to join the Derby. Also, I would have to quit school.

"Jewish boys don't do such things," my parents vehemently argued. "You're too young, and you're not out of school yet. No, you can't go."

When I threatened to run away, my parents agreed to sign. But they were also influenced by my promise to complete my schooling through correspondence courses, and by being assured there was strict adult supervision of all young skaters in the Derby.

Once it was all settled, Mom was supportive and became a fan. Before I left, she embroidered a blue Star of David on a white circle and sewed it to the front of my skating shorts. I wore it proudly.

The first time Mom saw me skate, it was in Los Angeles. I introduced her to the team and people in the front office, and took her to see our Olympic-style kitchen and meet our wonderful cook, Rosie.

Then I got Mom a good seat, in the front

BOB JOSEPH

ROLLER
SERIES 120
DERBY

DERBY DAREDEVIL
The author, who skated under the name of Bob Joseph, traveled all over the country in the '50s for $100 a week with all expenses paid. He's pictured on a 1950 Roller Derby postcard above, and on the far right in the photo at right.

S.F. BOMBERS---3-7-56

row, near the small stage where the Derby announcers and timer sat. When Mom saw me in my first jam of the night, getting blocked by two big guys from the opposing teams, she jumped up to the rail, raised her fists and yelled at the skaters to take it easy on "her boy."

Dick Lane, the famous television announcer ("Whoa, Nellie!"), saw my mom in action and asked to meet her. They got along so well that from then on, whenever we skated in Los Angeles, Dick would drive to my mother's apartment and take her to the Derby in his limousine. She was a celebrity on her block and loved every minute of it.

I skated all over the country, from Madison Square Garden in New York to the Coliseum in Chicago, Miami Stadium, the Cow Palace in San Francisco and the Rose Bowl in Pasadena.

And I skated with—and against —some of the Derby's all-time greats, such as Midge "Toughy" Brashun, "Crazy" Ann Calvello, Loretta "Little Iodine" Behrens, Elmer "Elbows" Anderson and many more.

The most fabulous skater I was fortunate to meet and skate against was "Slammin' Jammin'" Sammy Skobel. He was the fastest skater in the Derby and one of the higher scorers. That was all the more remarkable when I found out Sammy was legally blind from a childhood illness.

On the track, Sammy would grab your elbow and peer intently at your jersey to see if you were on his team or the opposition's. After leaving the Derby, Sammy taught himself to ski and play golf. He also opened a school in Mount Pleasant, Illinois, where he taught the blind and people with various disabilities how to ski and play golf.

When I skated with the Hollywood Ravens, we set up a Derby track in one of the big sound stages. It was perfect for televising the games and attracted plenty of movie stars. I remember seeing Cesar Romero, Ida Lupino, Howard Duff, Marilyn Maxwell and Craig Stevens.

I especially remember Michael Rennie, because I landed right on top of him one time when I got blocked over the rail. He was sitting cozily with two beautiful blond starlets.

I had just seen Mr. Rennie in the now classic science fiction movie *The Day the Earth Stood Still*. So I quickly came up with *"Klaatu barada nikto!"*, the command he gave his humanoid robot, Gort, in the movie.

I also apologized profusely. "I'm honored," Mr. Rennie said with a grin. "That's the first time anyone has gone to such an extreme just to get an autograph."

I left the Derby in 1956, settled down, got married and completed my education, earning a degree in computer science. I retired in 1995.

I had a great time while it lasted. But one thing I learned from being in the Roller Derby was to not volunteer too much information

to a new doctor. Why?

There was never enough room on the form to list my major injuries, which were: nose broken five times, both shoulders dislocated, breastbone separated from ribs, six broken ribs, every finger broken, several toes broken, elbow and knee bones chipped and a broken tailbone.

See what I mean?

HY JOSEPH SAN PEDRO, CA

DERBY MOM At first, Eva Joseph didn't want her boy in the Derby, but she became a fan. At left, Hy Joseph struck a "jammin'" pose at a reunion in Las Vegas in '95.

THOUGHT TO REMEMBER ─ Success consists of getting up just one more time than you've fallen down.

FUN & GAMES **101**

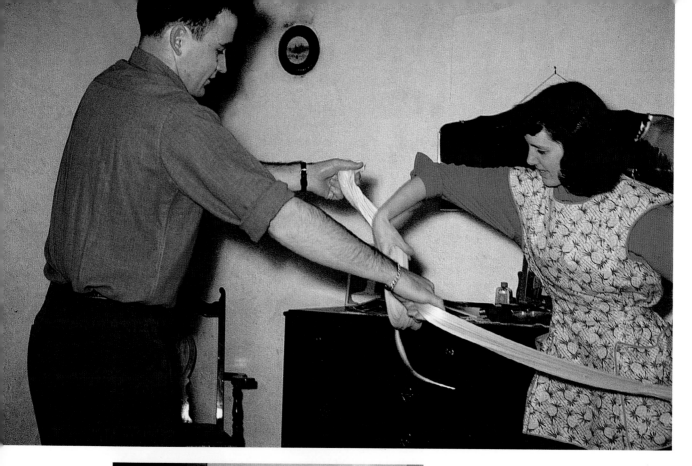

TUG O' WAR WITH TAFFY At this '50s taffy pull in Nampa, Idaho, the author is seen above (on the right) pulling with sister-in-law Wanda Agenbroad and below with neighbor Reva Clark. At top, Wanda and her husband, Larry, pulled.

MAKING "CLOTHESLINE" TAFFY WAS A SWEET JOB

Clothesline taffy! As I was growing up in the '30s, just mentioning the name to our family of seven kids filled the air with excitement.

Not only was taffy a treat, but it meant we'd have company at our New Mexico ranch. It took many hands to make this sticky specialty. And in the days before television, this was our entertainment.

We didn't have electricity back in the 1930s, so all cooking was done on our Majestic wood range. December through February was the optimum time for taffy, since keeping the stove hot for the candy helped heat the house. And we needed the cold weather outside to cure it.

In those days, we started with the basic ingredients—sugar, corn syrup, gelatin, paraffin and milk. We cooked the taffy until it was brittle in cold water, then poured it into a well-buttered sheet pan and set it out to cool.

Every few minutes, we'd knead it and try to work it into a ball. It was still very hot and took several tries to get it cool enough to be handled. Then, with well-buttered hands, the first pullers worked the candy together until they could form it into a rope and begin stretching it, a little at a time. It was important to run their hands the full length of the rope each time to work all of it and keep it intact.

Their hands got very warm, and we made sure more pullers were standing by with buttered hands to take over. As the taffy cooled, little strands would leave the main rope—and the children were there instantly, eager to catch the first piece.

As the taffy was pulled, it got harder, and the rope got very long. Sometimes you had to back up to be able to keep your feet anchored—especially if the person pulling on the other end was heftier.

The candy was light brown when we started and got lighter as it stretched. It was easy to get anxious and not keep on pulling. When it was ready, it had separated into several ropes, and running our hands over it wouldn't keep it together.

When it was as light as possible, we placed the strands on a clean sheet, then folded the sheet over the clothesline to harden, hence the name "clothesline taffy."

When it was completely cold, we could bring it in. It was now so brittle that placing the sheet on a hard surface would break the taffy into pieces. What was left after we all sampled our fill was placed in airtight containers.

These pictures show us making taffy in 1953 in Nampa, Idaho, after my husband, Stanley, and I were married and had small children. We all played games and snacked while the candy was cooking, making sure someone was always ready to take over stirring, a difficult and constant part of the process.

We loved having neighbors and family members come and join in the fellowship, pulling taffy…and making lots of great memories.
EVELYN AGENBROAD EMMETT, ID

▲ **EVERYBODY DANCE!**
"I lived in an apartment above the Arthur Murray Dance Studio on Walnut Street in Harrisburg, Pennsylvania," says Shirley Shaffer of Harrisburg. The dancers in this photo, taken in 1952 or 1953, taught students to rumba and cha-cha across the ballroom floor.

▲ **BOWLED OVER BY DUCKPINS**
Shirley Hammen (center), Nottingham, Maryland, was secretary of her duckpin league. "The balls and pins are smaller than those used in regular bowling," she says, recalling how her team, the Nite Owls, let the good times roll.

THOUGHT TO REMEMBER ▸ The time you enjoy wasting is not wasted time.

FUN & GAMES **103**

▲ FRIDAY NIGHT FIGHTS

"With money short in the 1940s, my parents, Arthur and Grace Genest, had people over for Friday night parties at their home in Manchester, New Hampshire," says Art Genest of Bedford. "Sometimes my brother Bill and I would provide the entertainment by putting on boxing gloves in the basement. Mom (on the right in the dark dress) was quite uneasy about the whole thing! We were pretty evenly matched, though. In 1945, when this photo was taken, Bill (the boxer on the left) was 9 and I was 10."

▲ SYNCHRONIZED FUN

"We four friends considered this our 'celebrity' photograph," says Barbara Kasmiroski of Waco, Texas. "Pictured in 1948 are (by their maiden names, from left) Freddie Ruth Little, Barbara Toney, Anne Parten and Mary Frances Parmley. When Garvin Rand built the roller-skating rink in Groesbeck, about 40 miles east of Waco, teenagers from the other small towns nearby would come to skate; the only other recreation was a movie. We became very good skaters."

▲ CONSTRUCTING CONFIDENCE

"My brother, Edwin (left), and I were residents of the Uhlich Orphan Home in Chicago from August 1932 until November 1940," writes Robert Schaeffer, Walkerton, Indiana. "We spent much of our time building model airplanes, footlockers and other wood projects and constructing kayaks to use at summer camp. Among other things, we learned carpentry and how to repair our own shoes during summers at Three Oaks Camp. What I learned at Uhlich served me well throughout my life and gave me the confidence to build my own home during the 1950s."

◄ HAVING A BOUNCING BALL

Kids looking for fun had the world on a string with a Hi-Li paddle in hand. "It looks like my sisters and cousins were seeing who could hit the ball the most times in a row without a miss," Greg Lopatka, Downers Grove, Illinois, says about the 1950s shot. "Standing, from left, are my sister Pat, my cousins Marcella and Josephine, my sister Mary and my cousin Frank. Lounging on the grass is my friend Bill Link."

Truly Amusing

An action-packed day at the fair, amusement park or zoo was so full of excitement...just thinking about it makes you want to grab the brass ring and do it all over again.

▲ BEARING UP NICELY

"The factory where my dad worked had a display at our county fair in the 1950s," writes Joyce Yoest Minnis, Conneaut Lake, Pennsylvania. "Wanting a photo for their newsletter, his co-worker posed me with two teddy bears. I wasn't happy when I learned I couldn't keep them! Over 50 years later, I wouldn't miss a day at the fair."

▲ ONE MERRY MAID

Local festivals in the good old days always had a kaleidoscope of color, sounds, aromas and laughs to entice young and old. Sitting high in the saddle aboard her brightly painted steed, this little blondie was all smiles on a merry-go-round in a delightful photograph from Bob Taylor of Cordell, Oklahoma.

▶ COTTON CANDY DANDIES

The food item of choice for this trio of sweet tooths was 100 percent cotton–candy, that is–at the Nebraska State Fair in this September 1962 picture shared by Hazel Magner, who lives in Omaha. Pictured, from left, are her sons, Roger and Jerry, and her husband, Jim.

THOUGHT TO REMEMBER ▸ Be a live wire and you won't get stepped on.

▲ CRACKERJACK OUTING

It was opening day in April 1964 when the McCluskey family attended the Milwaukee Braves game at Milwaukee County Stadium. Youngest son Bill (top, left with his stepmom, Jean, and dad, William) was a Dodgers fan, recalls his wife, Mary, of Colgate, Wisconsin. "He and his buddy Richard Hickey would take the bus to the games. When the Dodgers played, they'd wait outside the visitors' locker room to get players' autographs. Bill still has his autograph book. It's filled with names like those of Sandy Koufax, Don Drysdale and Maury Wills." The slide above shows Bill and older brother Mike with Jean.

◄ DAD, CAN WE GET ONE?

"My daughters, 2-year-old Carol and 1-year-old Norma (in both photos at left), were very taken with the polar bears at the John Ball Park Zoo," says Karl Lundeen of Grand Rapids, Michigan, where the zoo is still located. "We were at the zoo on a beautiful Sunday afternoon in the spring of 1963."

Outdoor Adventures

AN OUTSIDE CHANCE AT FUN

TRAVELING IN TANDEM

My wife, Barbara, and I enjoyed riding this unique 1929 Schwinn tandem bike, which I bought from Hanke's bike shop on Oakland Avenue in Milwaukee, Wisconsin.

Backseat driving was not a problem at all. See that chain running from the back fork to the front fork? That allowed the backseat rider to both pedal and steer.

When I rode the bike alone on the backseat, it was fun to watch the folks on our block stare in amazement.

This picture was taken in 1959 in front of our first small flat on North 40th Street. We kept the bike for about 10 years, and I gave rides to our children and many of the neighbor kids. They sat in front, often not reaching the pedals, and enjoyed the view while I played chauffeur.

HENRY ALTHOEN MILWAUKEE, WI

BEFORE BLAZE ORANGE

Every fall, my dad, William Mahan (below), took a week to go hunting around Erroll, New Hampshire. One year around 1948, he took me and Mom along.

Back then, hunters dressed in the traditional red and black plaid so they'd be more visible to other hunters and not be mistaken for game. I'm guessing Mom, who took the photo, picked out my wardrobe.

That's our Terraplane parked behind us. While Dad was out hunting, Mom and I were happy to hang out around the cabin.

WILLIAM MAHAN JR. WEST ROXBURY, MA

SUITED TO A TEE "Most Sunday afternoons, you could find my parents, Jean and Jeff Weston (far right), on a golf course with friends," says Sue O'Neill of Beatrice, Nebraska. "They lined up for this 1960 shot in Bemidji, Minnesota, where my family owned a summer cabin. My grandparents started going to beautiful Lake Bemidji in the '20s, and we still visit to this day."

BULL'S-EYE! "My parents, Margaret and Gerald Haywood, dabbled in archery," writes Richard Haywood from Laurel, Maryland. "In this slide, taken by my father in 1944 or '45, my mother is at a target they set up in the baseball field in Westport, Maryland. It was a paper mill town, and Dad was the director of research for the West Virginia Pulp and Paper Co., now MeadWestvaco Corp."

SERENITY OF A FISHERMAN "My late uncle, Lee H. Turner, enjoyed fishing on Lake Kushaqua, located near the town of Saranac Lake in Franklin County, New York, in 1961," says Lee H. Turner of Norwood.

THOUGHT TO REMEMBER ▶ Don't be concerned about the years in your life…rather the life in your years.

FUN & GAMES **109**

THE BALLOON BOOGIE? "My family members appear to be dancing while enjoying a lawn game," Helen Dankovich, Orchard Park, New York, says about this fun photo taken on July 9, 1967. They were practicing their fancy footwork in the backyard of her West Seneca home, where she lived for 30 years.

SNOW AND HONEY "A skirt and loafers didn't get in the way of my fashionable Aunt Honey's winter fun," writes Karen Bishop from New Brighton, Pennsylvania. "She was without a doubt the best-dressed sledder on this snowy day in Freedom, Pennsylvania. The photograph was taken in front of our family's store, DiSanzo's Market, back in the 1950s."

GOOD CATCH "When my family lived in Iowa, we took regular trips to my aunt's house in Minnesota," says Gloria James of Hacienda Heights, California. "My sister Charlotte Plunkett caught this impressive haul at Crystal Lake during one of our visits in the late 1940s or early '50s."

HAPPY LANDING "This photo of my mother, Viola Moreau, was taken near Hibbing, Minnesota, in January 1925," says Jacqueline Haskin of Northville, Michigan. "Several months later, she was amazed to see it on display in a photographer's shop window under the caption, 'What not to do when taking pictures.' Note the picture-taker's shadow in the lower left corner. It's my favorite shot of my mom anyhow."

CHAIN GANG OF PAINTERS "While visiting their grandparents, sisters Shirley (left) and Virginia Kompe got work painting power poles in the Miami area for Florida Power and Light, filling in for men who were serving in World War II," writes Virginia's husband, Irving Candee of Baldwinsville, New York. "Over the winter of 1944-'45, they raised ladders and hoisted the housings for the bases of the poles. They also served as 'grunts' for the linemen. This photo, taken for the *Miami Herald*, shows them in all their painted glory, checking their safety equipment."

CHAPTER 6

At Work

FOR GENERATIONS, PEOPLE HAVE KEPT OCCUPIED
IN SOME PRETTY REMARKABLE WAYS. IN OFFICES
AND FACTORIES, ON SALES ROUTES OR IN THE
AIR, THEY'VE MADE A LIVING AND A LIFE

Cooking Up Business
PUTTING FOOD ON THE TABLE

SEE YOU AT THE BARREL

The Barrel, a root beer and food stand built by my grandfather John Bryan in 1932, was a popular place in the 1930s and '40s. It was the only drive-in served by "curb girls" in our small town of 5,000. Food trays were secured to the tops of car windows with a brace.

My first job at the barrel-shaped food stand, which was bright orange with black metal bands, was "curb girling" and frying up the burgers and hot dogs, both selling for about 10 cents. (That's me, below, between my parents, Cec, in the striped dress, and Art.)

An all-time favorite of our customers was the Coney Island, a hot dog topped with our family's secret sauce and lots of ground onions and mustard or ketchup. *Mmm*, I can almost taste one now.

I believe it was Hires root beer that we served from a barrel inside the stand. Dad used to mix it up in large cans from syrup in our basement.

When Dad was out of town, it was Albert "Abie" Zavalney, our only male employee, who mixed the root beer. Abie was also the cook and our protector. We always made him deliver the trays to customers' cars in bad weather. A girl can't get her hair wet!

The daily arrival of the ice truck was a big event. The kids hanging around the Barrel at that time would beg Abie for ice chips that the iceman had chipped off from the frosty blocks with his pick. What a wonderful treat that was on a scorching North Dakota day!

Dad eventually built a kitchen on the back of the Barrel and added several booths to seat patrons who walked over from the movie theater a couple of blocks away. It was a large area to cover when everything was full, and we were tired at the end of a shift. The customers liked to sit and visit, so our summer days were long.

Those days ended when my parents sold the Barrel to a local couple in 1944.

In 1951, the Barrel was moved to New Town, North Dakota. The last time I passed our beloved drive-in, it was beginning to collapse from old age. It was sad to see, but there are so many wonderful (and delicious) stories that live on in my memory.

JEAN LINSKEY KAPP CASPER, WY

FRESHLY POPPED BY POP

As a young man just out of basic training at the end of World War II, my father-in-law, Robert Furgason (above), needed a job. Somehow, he decided to sell popcorn.

Building materials were hard to come by, so Dad made his wagon entirely out of recycled items. A Ping-Pong table became the floor, a Model T frame was the chassis, and the sides were made of Masonite walls with removable screens. A traveling sign painter added color and class for just $25.

Dad asked his Uncle Harry to co-sign a $100 loan for the popper and a peanut roaster. His first weekend, Dad made enough to pay back the loan. He sold his popcorn for 10 cents a small box, 25 cents for a family-size box.

Peanuts cost just 15 cents.

The wagon was movable, but it mostly stayed in one place—across from a park where dances and picnics were often held. On a busy night, Dad would make at least $100. His humble business, combined with the GI Bill and his day job at a lumberyard, paid his way through college.

EVA SMITH-FURGASON IRONWOOD, MI

"That's my future wife, Priscilla, in 1947, sprinkling water on fruits and vegetables at a busy produce stand she's tending with a young co-worker in York, Pennsylvania. Prices like those on the signs aren't often seen today!"

HAROLD MARTIN LITITZ, PA

LOVE TOOK SOME TIME TO BAKE

My mother felt crushed after having gone through a divorce, and the situation was made more dire by the Depression. She knew there would be no money coming from my father, and she had to do something fast.

Borrowing $700 from her father around 1936, my mother opened a grocery store in the Rosedale Park neighborhood of Detroit, Michigan. It was called the Rosedale Fenkell Market. (That's Mom, above, left, with her sister Olga Brunette.)

Mom got help from Olga, along with my younger brother, Nicky D'Arca, and me, ages 10 and 12. With the four of us working, we built up the business, and the store did well in the affluent area.

We sold just about everything in the store. Our pies came from the Acme Pie Co., and the deliveryman, Roy Mathews (inset), soon took a liking to Mom.

But Mom, fresh from the terrible failure of her first marriage, wanted nothing to do with the pie man, or any other man.

I liked Roy, though, especially when he'd take my brother and me out to his truck and tell us to pick out a pie for ourselves.

I loved pies, and these were the fresh ones that were delivered to restaurants. There were chocolate cream, coconut cream, banana cream, apple and more.

So I'd pick out a pie and take it into the store. But Mom would say, "No. Give it back."

I'd tell her Roy said I could have it. Mom would get upset with me and would say she did not want to be obligated to anyone.

Even though my aunt and I both liked Roy, who was such a sweetheart, Mom wouldn't give him the time of day.

Roy was persistent, though. When he got off work, he'd come to the store and help with things that were too hard for the two women to do.

If something broke down, Roy would fix it. He even helped my brother and me with our homework and fixed our bicycles.

The turning point came after a year or so, when Aunt Olga got sick. In a very short time, Olga died. Mom was devastated, fainting when she heard the bad news. She couldn't believe her sister was gone.

Mom and Olga were only two years apart. They had been very close and did everything together.

Mom became very depressed and grew even more dependent on Roy, who began doing a lot of the jobs Olga had done.

Roy also helped Mom out of her depression. He cheered her up and told her that she had two children to raise and support. He urged her to keep her chin up as she had before Olga's death, when they were doing so well.

Eventually, Mom began to see what a good guy Roy was and began to treat him so. When I was old enough to watch the store by myself, Mom and Roy finally started dating.

Roy won Mom's heart, and after they were married, he came to work at the store. He often joked that if he hadn't given me all those pies, he would not have been able to win Mom.

I often wonder just how many pies Roy gave me!

ANNE STANBROOK SAN CLEMENTE, CA

THOUGHT TO REMEMBER — Be exact in business, generous in friendship.

STARTING LINEUP "Notice how the lunch trays are ready for students in this early-1940s photo, along with the milk bottles, which were washed and returned for refilling," says Marie Murphy Garland of Nashville, Tennessee. "My mother-in-law, Jerdie Toler Garland (far right), worked in this cafeteria at Cockrill Elementary School in Nashville to occupy her time and mind, because she had four sons in the military during World War II."

SAILORS DROPPED ANCHOR AT BUD'S HOT HOUSE

While awaiting discharge from the Navy, where I'd served in the Atlantic and Mediterranean on the destroyer *USS Macomb*, I was sent to Camp Elliott, about 20 miles east of San Diego. We were allowed to work in town as civilians so long as we met muster at Camp Elliott. Fortunately, I got a job at Bud's Hot House.

Compared to the fast-food restaurants we see everywhere today, this little place was way ahead of its time. We served tamales, hot dogs, coffee, cold beverages and popcorn in a speedy two minutes.

This photograph was taken in November 1945. I'm the cook behind the counter (second from the right), standing next to the owner of the place, Bud Gallagher, originally from Denver. I shared a barracks with the other men in the shot, whom I knew only by their first names and home states.

Standing, from left, are Al from South Carolina, Bill of New Jersey and "Slim" from Texas.

GAYLE KRING MADISON, IN

Door-to-Door
OPPORTUNITY'S KNOCKING

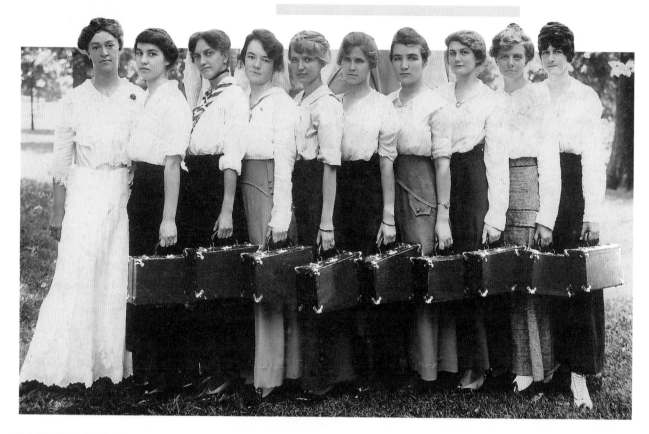

BAKING POWDER LADIES DIDN'T LOAF AROUND

My mom, Donna Eubanks Ward (above, second from right), became a demonstrator for the Calumet Baking Powder Co. in the early 1900s.

She married my dad, Orman Ward, in 1916. The Calumet demonstrators were not allowed to be married, so my parents kept their marriage secret until Mom became pregnant with my oldest sister in 1918.

She had four more children. Sadly, she died when I was 7.

Years later, I found a Calumet textbook from her working days. It's in pretty bad shape, but it's still fascinating.

The introduction explains the mission of the Calumet demonstration ladies.

"There are millions of smart women who use Calumet daily because they know its goodness. There are others who have never used it, because they have had no opportunity to learn of its superior quality.

"You are to call on these housewives and show them Calumet Baking Powder exactly as it is. You are to tell the truth and nothing but the truth. You are to tell them what Calumet is and show them what Calumet will do."

The pocket-size book gave instructions for putting on demonstrations, complete with prepared speeches, and showed the demonstrators how to keep records of sales.

Suggestions from the book included these sales techniques:

• Don't talk so fast. You waste time and energy if the lady does not understand what you say.

• When working big homes in the elite district, ask for the butler or the cook. The cook does most of the buying and is the one you must convince.

• You will find a few families who don't bake. They buy bread, cakes and pastry at the stores because it is so convenient. The chances are they are poor cooks. Show them how easy it is to bake delicious food with Calumet.

• If you demonstrate properly and make your customer understand what a great help the powder will be, the order will be given without solicitation.

IDA PALUSKU COLORADO SPRINGS, CO

SNACK HAPPY "My dad, V.V. Atchley (second from right), worked 30 years as a salesman for Lance baked goods," writes Danny Atchley of Mineral Wells, Texas. "The company, which has been going strong for more than 100 years, flourished in the hard days of the Depression because folks could afford to buy its low-priced goods, such as 5-cent packages of peanut butter crackers."

BRUSHING UP ON SALES TACTICS "This 1946 photo was taken when my mother, Kathryn Betcher (right), from Osco, Illinois, sold Fuller Brush products," says Janelle Schmedt of Cambridge. "With her is friend and partner Jeannette Talaga from Moline. Mom was a hardworking lady, growing up on a farm in the Depression and later becoming a successful businesswoman. She and husband Harold acquired several farms and apartments. She raised 600 chickens each year and had a large egg route. She was also very involved in church and ladies' groups and still found time to raise her two daughters."

MEDICINE MAN "My brother, John (above), worked as a salesman for this company when we lived in Hollis, Oklahoma," writes Jim Copeland of Detroit, Texas. "I don't remember much about John's route. I think this picture was taken at a customer's house around 1917. In 1924, when I was 14, I lived with my sister and her husband on their farm on the plains of West Texas."

CUSTOMERS FLOCKED TO HIS COWBELL "In 1910, my grandfather Arthur A. Lynd—Shorty Daddy to us—was about 18 years old and living along the Gulf Coast of Mississippi," says Clara Williford, Heflin, Louisiana. "He worked for a butcher, Mr. Seymour, selling meat from a wagon (above). Whenever Shorty Daddy made a stop, he would ring a cowbell to let customers know he was there. Then he'd jump down from the wagon, hurry to the back and open the doors to shoo away all the flies before anyone got there. He later became a butcher himself and worked until 1962, when he retired at the age of 70."

IT'S ELECTRIC!

In the late 1930s and early '40s, electricity was finally coming to rural northwest Arkansas. My grandmother Edna Henbest was hired by the federal Rural Electrification Administration to contact every rural household in two counties for a study to determine who wanted power lines run to their homes.

The government later hired Grandma to help run a small REA office and to promote the use of electricity by way of home demonstrations. It was pretty much a given that if electric appliances could replace wood-burning cookstoves, the woman of the house would quickly see to it that power came to her kitchen! This picture of Grandma was taken in 1944 in her demonstration kitchen.

ROGER DENNINGTON LOGANVILLE, GA

THOUGHT TO REMEMBER ~ Small opportunities are often the beginning of great enterprises.

A REGAL GIFT

My father, Fern Regal, was a natural salesman and entrepreneur.

Born in 1885 in Fowler, Ohio, he grew corn and sold it as popcorn when he was 12. He even sold dustpans door-to-door for 25 cents apiece. One customer bought two because she said his spiel was so effective.

After my mother, Frances Goe, married my dad in 1914, they took a train to Florida for their honeymoon. Ever the salesman, my father sold Fuller brushes during the honeymoon.

Later, they moved to Ashtabula, Ohio, and bought a two-story house on Main Street. There he opened the Regal Sales Agency, devoting an area on the first floor to selling Royal vacuum cleaners and keeping the books. Sometimes, he delivered machines by bike. Later, he added washing machines, irons, refrigerators and ranges to his line. As a child, I helped out in the sales room.

Folks in town trusted my father. As he would walk down a street, someone would yell, "Hey, Regal, send me out a washer," without even asking about the price. Some customers came to our house and made payments along with a little interest, but Dad's favorite arrangement was bartering.

He bartered appliances for honeycombs from a beekeeper, milk from two brothers who owned a dairy, and gas from a customer who ran a filling station.

Over many years, my father and his salesmen sold an enormous number of Royal vacuum cleaners. In recognition of his salesmanship, the folks at Royal paid Dad the ultimate honor. They named a new brand of vacuum cleaner after him—the Regal!

Years later, my husband and I were in a hotel in Paris when we saw an employee cleaning the lobby with a Regal vacuum cleaner. We couldn't help but feel proud of my father, who'd achieved a small measure of fame for his uncanny sales skills.

MIRIAM MULLINS ST. PETERSBURG, FL

A REGAL GIFT
Fern Regal (below in 1923) personally delivered vacuums and other appliances from his home-based headquarters.

Parts and Labor

They say a little hard work never hurt anyone. And as these reader photos show, dedication, gumption and elbow grease are exactly what's needed to turn the key to success.

▲ NEED A LIFT?

"My father, Anthony Palazzi, the second man from the right, is standing next to Burt Kemmerling, the owner of this Cleveland, Ohio, car dealership," Fran Segulin from Macedonia says about this 1949 photo of eight Fords up on hydraulic racks. "Dad became one of its top mechanics, and customers would ask for him by name. His pride and joy was a 1936 Ford Roadster convertible. He built it from the ground up with car parts from the junkyard and any that were discarded at work."

◄ NO GLASS CEILING HERE

"In 1978, I became the first female lineman in Columbus, Georgia, climbing telephone poles for Southern Bell (now AT&T)," writes Diane Strawn Hoyle of Hamilton. "Safety belts and hooks minimized the risk of falling, but concentration was essential. It helped that I was strong, because the cables and equipment were heavy. I took a lot of pride in my work."

▲ IT ALL CAME OUT IN THE WASH

"I got this 1935 photo from a lady whose grandmother worked at the Chicago Maytag plant pictured," says Larry Fast of Salem, Oregon. "Workers on the assembly line turned out tub after tub of the labor-saving machines. These Maytags had wheels and could be easily rolled to the next station. I'm sure many a homemaker praised the day her very own Maytag arrived!"

◀ GREEN MACHINES

Before email, text messaging and overnight FedEx deliveries, smartly uniformed delivery boys—like the ones shown here in downtown Cleveland, Ohio—relied on fleets of sturdy bicycles and pedal power to deliver telegrams and other communications. "These boys worked for the Postal Telegraph Co., where my father was an office manager until about 1939," writes Bob Gazso of North Olmsted. "This photograph was taken in 1936. I heard the office also had a marching band that took part in local parades."

All in a Day's Work

PRIDE AND A PAYCHECK

SECRETARY BOOT CAMP

Career choices were limited for a young woman in the early 1960s. I found secretarial work more enticing than nursing or teaching, and in my senior year of high school, I was selected to attend the best secretarial school of the day: the Katharine Gibbs School. Once my acceptance letter arrived, I was headed into the heart of New York City!

My dorm was the Barbizon Hotel for Women. Katharine Gibbs had reserved several floors of this grand hotel just for its students, as well as a private dining room.

I had my own room, too, with a colorful bedspread, matching curtains and a desk with a typewriter. After my mother helped me unpack, she went back home to Ithaca, and I was on my own for the first time in my life. It wasn't long before I met a bubbly redhead named Connie from Ohio. We became close friends and fierce competitors.

Each morning, I would put on my business suit and hurry out the door to catch the bus. Classes were held in the upper level of Grand Central Station. We Gibbs girls stood out from our peers. We were the only girls our age carrying briefcases and wearing hats and white gloves. (That's me in required attire, below, left.)

For lunch, Connie and I would get 15-cent hot dogs from a street vendor. Then it was back to class and hours of shorthand and typing practice (below, right).

When we came back home, we were in so much pain from our high heels that we'd take them off the minute the bus pulled away and limp to the hotel. After dinner came the grueling homework. But we did make time for exploring the city and strolling in Central Park.

The school year ended as the certification process began. This was a series of difficult exams covering everything we'd studied. Connie and I whizzed through and were among the first group to be certified.

Although there were plenty of prestigious employers in New York City, I returned to Ithaca and took my first secretarial job at Cornell University.

The days of being a polished secretary have faded away, but it was fun while it lasted.

MILLIE PIRKO TRIFF HANCOCK, NY

· APR · 63

TIMES HAVE CHANGED

About 75 years ago, my father, Sid Salzman, began his career as a pharmacist on Long Island. Dad (above) needed to know how many hours a week the New York State Pharmaceutical Association permitted pharmacists to work.

After my father's move to an assisted living facility, I came across the reply—from May 25, 1940—that Dad received from the association's secretary. The man, Robert S. Lehman, pointed out that the allowable 132 hours for two weeks "makes only 66 hours a week average."

The man considered this to be really quite reasonable, considering the hours he put in when starting his career as a pharmacist, back in 1895.

"When I was a young man, some 45 years ago," Lehman wrote, "I was glad to work for $20 a week, with 13 hours a day and one day off each week. I put in 78 hours a week and slept behind the store, and it did not hurt me physically, financially, professionally nor socially.

"But times have changed," he admitted.

If only he knew!

STAN SALZMAN FAIR OAKS, CA

AN INDEPENDENT WOMAN

My beautiful sister Marjorie Palmer O'Neill went to radio school at East Carolina University after graduating from high school in 1942. With her skills, she had her pick of jobs. But Marjorie had a mind of her own, so she went by herself to Washington, D.C., and got a job at the Naval Research Laboratory. Marjorie, who met her husband at the lab, has always defied the odds. For example, when her husband wouldn't teach her to drive, she took in sewing to pay for lessons. In this 1945 photo, Marjorie is leaning against the very large computer she used to do her work (it was an experimental model). Though she wouldn't talk about her job—things were secretive during and after World War II—she worked for 32 years at the lab, which is the research arm of the Navy. Looking at the size of Marjorie's cumbersome computer, I can't help but wonder at today's laptops and smartphones!

CAROLE PALMER LENOIR, NC

OUR *CINEMA PARADISO*

My father, Al Laurice, an Italian immigrant, worked in the movie industry all his life.

At age 20, he got his start with the Famous Players-Lasky Corp., which became Paramount Pictures. Then he took a sales job with 20th Century Fox.

Eventually, Dad took over the movie theater in Palo Alto and built a reputation for providing sophisticated entertainment to the Stanford University community.

In 1954, when I was about 6, Dad won a lawsuit against Palo Alto's Advisory Board of Commercial Amusements, a group of citizens who reviewed films and rated them for content or banned them entirely. His case cited the '52 U.S. Supreme Court ruling that the First Amendment protected motion pictures. Palo Alto's board was soon abolished.

My memories are mostly of the fun I had stretching out in the front row to watch movies, eating and drinking all the popcorn and cherry Coke I could consume.

Dad was a quiet, mellow guy, so I was surprised and proud to learn years later that he had stood up to censorship.

WENDY HORTON ROHNERT PARK, CA

"The Red Cross office in Portland, Oregon, had the very latest equipment in the '40s. That's my aunt, Mary Beagle, operating the big board with a smile, as a couple of Red Cross officials look on."

JANICE ROBB VANCOUVER, WA

HIGH-FLYING PIONEER "At a time when pilots were considered glamorous daredevils, my dad, Malvin Sellmeyer, called himself a 'glorified bus driver,'" says Jean Sellmeyer Smith, Crowley, Louisiana. "He was one of the first pilots hired by Braniff Airways in 1935. And his stunt-flying license was signed by Orville Wright! Dad's first route, from Dallas to Oklahoma City, was a puddle jump compared to modern flights. But to me, those early pilots were as brave as today's astronauts. It was a kick for me (above, right) to watch America's airline industry soar."

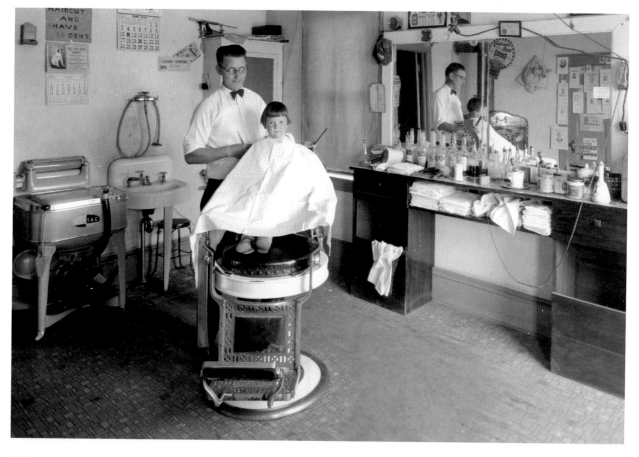

HAIR'S A FAMILY AFFAIR

A visit to the barbershop could be an adventure for the barber's daughter in 1934. The well-groomed lass in this photo is my future mother-in-law, Joyce Bjerk Jacobson, then 3, with her father, Oscar Bjerk, the barber in Karlstad, Minnesota, for many years. Joyce recalls being her dad's favorite guinea pig for trying out new products.

Note the price of 50 cents for a haircut and shave and the state-of-the-art Maytag washing machine. There are all sorts of advertisements for hair care products, an almanac, a sign reading "Scissors Sharpened Here," as well as an invitation to an American Legion picnic in Lancaster. On the shelves are Healox items and other products, an antiseptic sterilizer and a National Cash Register. The barber chair is from the Theo A. Kochs Co. of Chicago.

Oscar eventually closed his shop and moved to Minneapolis. The building was demolished a long time ago, but the snippets of memories remain.

BERTHA JACOBSON SAN ANTONIO, TX

THOUGHT TO REMEMBER ↝ You can't get much done by starting tomorrow.

Odd Jobs
IT'S BUSINESS AS UNUSUAL

I MISS THE CAT CALLS

Things were pretty tame around our house—until my dad became a lion tamer.

One summer morning in 1937, a crate addressed to my dad, George Keller, arrived, labeled with the message: "Here, Keller. Train this." In it was Simba, a mountain lion cub sent to Dad from Arizona by a fraternity brother. Thus was born Keller's Jungle Killers.

We lived outside of Bloomsburg, Pennsylvania, and until that day, life was fairly quiet. My mother, Eleanor, stayed home and took care of my baby sister, Katie, and me, age 9. Dad was an artist and headed the Department of Fine Arts at our local college.

As soon as Simba arrived, though, Dad devoured books on training wild cats. He believed whips, blank guns and chairs should be used only in emergencies. Instead, he trained his cats by using hand gestures, with Strauss waltzes as background music. Soon, Simba was walking a tightrope.

When World War II started, Dad hit the road. He went into debt to buy a used two-pole tent, two more mountain lions and an African lion named Regal. As more bookings came, more animals joined the show. In the winter, Dad and his menagerie would return to our house. In the spring, a caged arena in our backyard became a training area. Hordes of friends and townspeople came to watch.

As time passed, the bookings increased. Dad went from grandstand acts at fairs to seasons with Shrine circuses, Ringling Bros. and Barnum & Bailey and even bookings at Disneyland.

The last time I saw Dad's act was in 1960 at Madison Square Garden. A few months later, he died of a heart attack during a show, surrounded by the animals we all loved. For our family, it had truly been a life beyond our wildest dreams.

JANE KELLER SNYDER BLOOMSBURG, PA

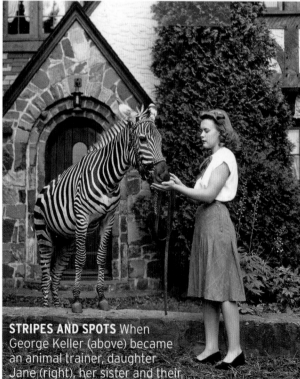

STRIPES AND SPOTS When George Keller (above) became an animal trainer, daughter Jane (right), her sister and their mom adopted his exotic tastes.

BUSTER'S ORDERS

As a student at California's Santa Monica City College in 1948, I'd go swimming once a week at the Chase Hotel.

One evening, a lifeguard at the pool told me that film star and swimming champ Buster Crabbe was planning a traveling water show, with tryouts scheduled for Easter break. I really wanted to give them a whirl since, at age 19, I'd never been outside California. So I worked hard on my strokes and form, and made the cast.

After many rehearsals, Buster Crabbe's Aqua Parade of 1948 opened at an arena in St. Louis. As I excitedly entered our dressing room, I noticed that on each mirror was a reminder: "Smile!"

Also at my spot was a lovely corsage box, which prompted the other girls to jeer, "Boy, you're a fast worker!" and "Who sent that?"

With great curiosity, I opened the box. There before me was a pair of foam rubber falsies! The "gift" came with a note, signed by Buster himself, that said simply: "Wear 'em."

MEREDITH MANNING HATHAWAY
OROVILLE, CA

POOL CUTIES
Aquatic beauties: (front, from left) Peggy Thigh, author Meredith Manning and Betty Cowan; (back, from left) Francima Fulton, Betty Hansen and CeCe McVay

---

THOUGHT TO REMEMBER ► Don't just entertain ideas…put them to work.

GRANDPA CARVED OUT A DUTCH TRADITION

When my grandpa John Kamphuis came to America from Holland as a young man, he brought with him his skill at making wooden shoes. Throughout his life, he made hundreds of pairs by hand to supplement his income.

As a young boy, I loved to watch him shave those pieces of poplar wood into the shape of a shoe, then drill them out and sand them by hand before embossing small decorations on them. It took about three hours to make a pair, which he sold for 40 cents to $1.15, depending on the size.

Grandpa lived in Englewood, a Chicago suburb that was home to several Dutch families, many of whom bought shoes he made in his garage workshop (above, right). In 1933, he was invited to demonstrate wooden shoe making at the 1934 World's Fair in Chicago (above, middle).

When the fair opened, he had several hundred pairs ready, but they sold out within two weeks of the opening. Grandpa ended up taking orders and making wooden shoes for more than a year after the fair closed.

My grandmother wore wooden shoes on washday, and they did a good job of keeping her feet dry when she hung clothes outside.

They were noisy to wear and not very comfortable, but Grandma said her feet got used to them. I never wore them, although I still have a few pairs of Grandpa's handiwork (above, left). I cherish them and the work ethic that special man taught me.

GERALD MULDER DURANGO, CO

ANCIENT ART—MODERN MIRACLE "That's how the Winfield China Co. labeled this marketing photo of my friend Aurora 'Dottie' Ontiveros painting a plate with the Passion Flower pattern in Santa Monica, California, in 1960," writes Mollie Bowling of Los Angeles. "To promote the product, sets of Winfield China were given to winners on the *Queen for a Day* television program."

MEMORIES TOOK OFF "I was lucky to be hired as a stewardess by United Air Lines in 1940," says Teddy Larson Frye, La Porte, Indiana. "I earned $125 a month, and we were like family. I stayed a year and a half, until I married. Back then, stewardesses had to be single. I have a scrapbook full of kind notes from passengers."

ALL HANDS ON DECK Getting the boys back from "over there" after World War II was an immense undertaking. The *USS Lew Wallace*, shown here with its decks crowded with military personnel, was among the Liberty ships that carried troops home. The October 1946 picture is shared by Lester Eckert of Millstadt, Illinois. He is one of the GIs (see second row from the back, fourth from the left) happy to have arrived in Seattle, Washington.

CHAPTER 7

True Patriots

WHEN DUTY CALLED, MILLIONS OF MEN AND
WOMEN ANSWERED—GIVING THEIR ALL
FOR THEIR COUNTRY. FROM OVER THE SEAS
AND ON THE HOMEFRONT, THEIR PERSONAL
REFLECTIONS SERVE AS PROUD REMINDERS

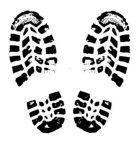

Boot Camp
RECRUITS GOT MARCHING ORDERS

DUCK AND ROLL

My father, William Beegle, faced his final test flight as a cadet in training at aviation school in Santa Maria, California, in 1943. He would have to fly an open cockpit Stearman aircraft while an instructor monitored him from the backseat.

During the flight, the instructor told Dad to do a slow roll. My dad maneuvered the airplane, but felt a pull on the talking tube midway through. Back then, there were no fancy radios or intercoms for pilots to use for communication. Instead, a rubber tube connected the teacher's speaking port to the cadet's helmet.

When Dad came out of the roll, he looked in the rearview mirror to see what had happened, only to discover that his flight instructor was missing! Had his teacher fallen out of the plane? Not only was he concerned for the safety of the instructor, but how could he land and explain what had happened? Now he would never graduate to become a pilot. Dad flew around and around, looking down at the ground in search of a parachute, but couldn't see a thing.

After a couple of minutes of panic, Dad checked the mirror again. This time he saw the instructor sitting in the backseat, laughing his head off. He had ducked down during the roll and pulled on the tube to pretend he had fallen out of the plane.

He'd been there the entire time.

When they landed, the flight instructor told Dad not to mention the prank so he could play the same trick on the next unsuspecting student. Later, Dad asked the instructor how the cadet after him had reacted.

"That guy never even missed me!" he said.

Dad graduated from aviation school with flying colors and became a B-17 pilot. For fun, at age 87, he got back in the cockpit. What a thrill it was to take control of a Stearman aircraft again after 68 years! The ride brought back a lot of memories, and this time, Dad made sure the instructor was safe in his seat.

CHRISTINE BEEGLE BLAIRSTOWN, NJ

GOING UP Cadets pose in formation in front of a Stearman aircraft in 1943 (right); William Beegle is second from the right. Above, William and his crew celebrate after his flight in 2011.

DROP AND GIVE ME KISSES

Anticipation swept through the ranks of my Marine Corps unit one June afternoon in 1959. I was one of 61 recruits of Platoon 337 assembled at boot camp in San Diego, California, and it was time for mail call.

When your name was called, you yelled, "Here, sir," executed a smart right face, double-timed to the end of your row, made two quick left turns, and continued at double-time speed toward the drill instructor. The DI held the letter in front of him, and you clamped the letter in your hands, continuing back to the formation.

Everything was fine until one recruit, Cliff, had the letter snatched back by the DI. On the back of the envelope was a red lipstick impression. The DI threw the letter on the ground. He then instructed Cliff to do push-ups and, when in the down position, to kiss the back of the envelope. Cliff was to keep this up until he opened the letter with a kiss because, after all, it had been sealed with one.

That night, all of us wrote to our girlfriends: *Under no circumstances are you to write anything other than your name and address on that envelope!* I wrote to my girlfriend, Sue Graefe of Sheboygan, Wisconsin, now my wife of many happy years.

RICHARD STRYSICK FARMINGTON, MN

ONE WAY TO DITCH YOUR SERGEANT

We knew we were good at marching after seven weeks of basic training at the WAC training center in Fort Lee, Virginia (below).

So, as we marched back to the barracks from the parade field one spring morning in 1954, we were pretty proud of ourselves.

Our drill sergeant saw a group of trainees beside the road taking a break from their classes. She decided to show us off a bit.

Walking backward, she commanded, "By the left flank, march!" We all turned smartly.

Then she called out, "By the right flank, mar…!" and suddenly disappeared!

She'd fallen into a drainage ditch. We could hardly keep from laughing as our muddy sergeant brought us to a halt.

MARILYN FERRARIS MELBOURNE, FL

▼ HEADSTANDING AT ATTENTION

"My husband, Howard 'Hap' Arnold (on his head in foreground), and his buddies found time to goof around at Marine boot camp in Parris Island, South Carolina, in 1953," writes Coralee Arnold of Cool, California. "He was in the Marines for about 20 years."

STIR-CRAZY When the author's class finished Army cooking school (she's seated on the left), they thought they'd be off to a mess hall. They went to a hospital instead.

COOKING SCHOOL GRAD ENDED UP IN SURGERY

Fresh from college with a degree in home economics in 1943, I thought an Army kitchen was the place for me. After basic training at Fort Oglethorpe, Georgia, I was sent to Cooks and Bakers School on the same post.

Being a coal miner's daughter from Pennsylvania, I felt at home with the coal-fired cast-iron stove. We had a walk-in refrigerator but no freezer. Ice came in huge blocks. There were no electric mixers, and our rolling pin was a mop handle that some genius had cut in half and smoothed to a velvet finish. You could roll four pie crusts at a time with it.

After two more months at Oglethorpe, we graduated—in my case, 15 pounds heavier.

Fifteen of us cooks were sent to Kennedy General Hospital in Memphis, Tennessee. The hospital already had experienced civilian cooks, so we were put on standby for new orders. Meantime, we volunteered as "fetchers and toters" at the 3,500-bed hospital.

That must have given the Army an idea, because the next thing we knew, we were sent to the Army and Navy Teaching Hospital in Hot Springs, Arkansas, and trained to be medics!

There is a similarity between a cook and a medical technician. Both wear white uniforms and work at tables with knives and saws. Both need patience (or patients) and require clean hands.

I later returned to Kennedy General to spend my Army career in operating rooms as a surgical technician. Surprisingly, I loved the job and was good at it.

So that's how a home-ec graduate, trained as a cook, became a medic. Still, that wasn't as drastic a change as my brother-in-law endured. A restaurateur in civilian life, the Army turned him into a chaplain's assistant!

NORA McCULLOCH-ROSDAHL
FORESTVILLE, PA

BY LAND AND SEA "This 1955 photo (right), taken about a year after the Korean War cease-fire, shows the 1st Marine Division getting ready for transport," writes John Wilson (left) of Medford, Oregon. "I served in Marine Observation Squadron 6, and all our supplies and aircraft had to be loaded onto Navy ships anchored off the port city of Inchon. Three weeks later, I was in San Diego greeting my wife and baby son!"

STANDING TALL "My dad, Bill Brown Jr., served in the Army Air Corps during World War II and flew a C-47 aircraft, dropping paratroopers on D-Day," writes William F. Brown III, from Nebo, North Carolina. "Dad was the tallest man in his squadron, and his best friend, Jack Kaminski, was the shortest. As you can see in this photo, they made quite a pair!"

THIS IS NO BROWNIE "My father-in-law, George Yagle, was a photographic lab technician with the Army Air Corps in Italy in 1942-'43," says Walter Moon, Reisterstown, Maryland. "He developed film, printed photographs and installed cameras in bombers."

THOUGHT TO REMEMBER ～ Our greatest triumph is rising every time we fall.

FEB 13 1953 KOREA

CLOSE QUARTERS

Hawkeye's tent on *M*A*S*H* was called the Swamp; we dubbed ours the Tee Hee Ranch. An earlier occupant's name inspired the moniker. Because all his equipment was marked "T. Heamon"—pronounced "Tee Hee-Man"—my tent mates and I decided to adopt the nickname for our abode at Kimpo Air Base during the Korean War.

Our tents slept nine men: eight on cots on the inside perimeter and one in the middle for the newest arrival. The new guy had no wall or shelf space for storage, so he had to live out of his footlocker until someone was transferred or sent home.

My buddies and I took this photograph on Feb. 13, 1953, five months before hostilities ended. (I'm seated second from the

left). That winter the temperature dropped so low that our fuel turned to slush overnight.

We were supposed to take turns going outside to shake the fuel drum, but we younger guys would pretend to be in a deep sleep, so beleagured Sgt. Weaver (standing) had to wake up to do it. In the morning, he always had loud words of complaint.

CHET CUTSHALL WILLOWICK, OH

THOUGHT TO REMEMBER ⤙ Injustice anywhere is a threat to justice everywhere.

BICYCLING WAC WAS TAKEN FOR A SURPRISE RIDE

As children, my sister and I would beg our parents for quarters so we could rent bicycles to ride in New York City's Central Park.

Ten years later and 1,500 miles from home, those rides came back to me, and I wished I had a bicycle to ride again. However, on a World War II Army post in Rantoul, Illinois, far from any sizable city, the car was king.

As a technical sergeant in charge of the Training Film Library at Chanute Field, I was entitled to an assigned vehicle, but every car, jeep, truck and bike had already been assigned.

Luckily, I discovered a bulletin board ad that said, "Bicycle For Sale—Good Condition—$17." The bike's red paint was a bit thin and rust was making inroads, but I was in seventh heaven.

Over the next few days, I whizzed around the post flaunting my wheels.

On the fourth day after my acquisition, I left my office and found that my trusty bike was missing! All the people I talked to protested their innocence or just sadly shook their heads and sympathized.

About three weeks later, the new ratings were announced, and I was promoted to master sergeant. After morning mess, I strolled to my office when

something caught my eye—it was my beautiful red bike, only better.

The red enamel shone and the chrome gleamed. The seat was neatly upholstered with thick foam rubber, and handsome handmade saddlebags with steel snaps hung from the rear fender.

On one saddlebag was painted the cartoon symbol from one of our B-24s, *The Redheaded WAC*. The other bore a replica of my master sergeant's stripes.

Tears were streaming down my cheeks as I became aware of a cluster of GIs gathered around me. Several sergeants explained how they made the seat from an old parachute pack, had snaps put on the saddlebags at the post's sheet metal shop, dipped the spokes and handlebars in chrome and spray-painted and baked the bicycle frame.

What a great bunch of guys. No wonder we won the war!

ANNE LEE DONIGER
POMPANO BEACH, FL

DESPERATE MEASURES FOR DUSTY TIMES

My Army training with the 818th Anti-Aircraft Artillery Battalion in 1943 included excursions to Fort Irwin, a sprawling and infernally hot training center in California, to fire a 40 mm cannon.

One time, we were led 17 miles deep into the Mojave Desert, where we lived in pup tents—we liked to call them posh apartments for two—for a long month and a half.

That's me (left) shaving outside

my tent. The blowing sand and soaring temperatures made staying clean a real challenge—until one clever GI Joe built a shower using an ammunition box, a rope and a bucket. The blazing desert sun warmed the water in the bucket, and each bather was allotted one bucketful. Pull the rope, wet and lather. Pull the rope again, rinse. No need for shower curtains, as we were 30 miles or more from civilization.

LAWRENCE R. CAYTON
FOND DU LAC, WI

We Can Do It!

From buying war bonds to making parts for fighting machines, the folks back home all proudly pulled together to encourage their troops over there until the victory was won.

◄ AIR AND SEA SHELLS
"I'm on the right, fifth from the front, with co-workers at Green River Ordnance Plant near Amboy, Illinois, in 1943," says Dorothy Gaffron of Taylorville, Illinois. "We made armor-piercing shells and helped in the area where the projectiles were loaded with explosives. Work went on around the clock. We knew the brave fellows on the front lines certainly had no holidays."

IT TAKES A VILLAGE ➤
"My mother-in-law, Betty Meyers (see arrow), was 19 in 1942, when her fiance, Ernest Wittkopf, began serving in the Navy," writes Forrest Plesko, Denver, Colorado. "She joined this large female welding crew at the Walter Butler shipyard in her hometown, Superior, Wisconsin. Butler produced 52 Liberty-type ships for the Marine Corps. On the photo, Betty wrote that she worked with a 'swell gang.'"

THOUGHT TO REMEMBER ➤ Our duty is not to see through one another, but to see one another through.

◄ BONDING TIME
"Mom (Marge) and Dad (Mal) both worked at the Douglas Aircraft Co. in Long Beach, California, where they met and fell in love in 1943," says Suzanne Gilbert of Portland, Oregon. "A month after their April 1944 wedding, while they were buying war bonds, a photographer snapped this publicity shot."

▲ GOING GREAT GUNS "My mother, Myrtle Glenna Stillions (far right), is working on this gun assembly line in 1942 or '43 at the Fairfax Bomber Plant in Kansas City, Kansas," writes Gwendolyn Mace of Raymore, Missouri. "She also installed the guns in the planes. Her younger sister, Mildred Bell, bucked rivets at the plant. General Motors took the place over for Chevrolet production after the war."

HOME OF THE BRAVE ▶
"Our little patriot Butchie shows off his Stars and Stripes as he prepares to fly the American flag in memory of all the selfless servicemen and women who sacrificed their lives for our country," writes Bill Larson of Batavia, Illinois.

◀ THE CHIN-UP GIRL
"During basic training in 1944, I entered my mom, Eulelia, in a contest to find America's 'Chin-Up Girl,'" says George T. McDaneil of Cordova, Tennessee. "My letter explained how Mom watched all five of her sons go to war, worked six days a week and, on weekends, invited wounded soldiers into our home. I wasn't surprised when she was chosen. Her story made national news. Besides winning a trip to Atlantic City, Mom met several celebrities, helped raise more than $1 million and inspired military mothers everywhere."

▲ LOOK UP IN THE SKY

"I'm the 13-year-old pointing out a plane on an observation tower in West Linn, Oregon, about 11 miles south of Portland, in 1942," says Charles Day of Boise, Idaho. "The walls inside the tower were covered with silhouettes of all kinds of aircraft. Anyone on the tower, which was manned 24 hours a day, needed to be able to identify any aircraft that came into view and report it to military headquarters. The photo was featured in Portland's major daily newspaper, *The Oregonian*."

◄ VIVE LA FRANCE!
Soldier Mark Gryska (right) of New Hartford, New York, set his camera on a timer to snap himself and his buddy Jack Swerer when Paris was liberated in 1944.

Entertaining the Troops

AN ALL-STAR SHOW OF SUPPORT

"ANCHORETTES" AWAY!

When I turned 18, during World War II, I joined a group called the Detroit Navy Anchorettes as the solo lyric soprano. You had to have someone in your family in the service to join. We entertained troops at camps and also sang at veterans hospitals.

In this picture from 1946, I'm standing outside at the front of the bus. The photo was taken at the Allen Park Veterans Administration Hospital, also referred to as Dearborn VA Hospital.

Our attire ranged from crisp uniform-like suits and hats trimmed with the Navy's anchor insignia to formal dresses worn when we performed in concerts.

Other girls I knew would say, 'What a way to meet guys,' but I had to laugh because the bus took us straight to the military camp. From there, we went directly onstage to perform, then back to the bus, rarely talking to the troops. In our spare time, we sold poppies and war bonds for the Allied cause and visited with veterans, hoping to cheer them up.

When the Anchorettes weren't on the road, we'd sing on Saturdays with a band of Army personnel for a program called *The Command Cavalcade*, which was aired on Detroit, Michigan, radio station WWJ.

CARRIE MROZ RIO RICO, AZ

DRUMMED INTO THE SERVICE

As one of the first U.S. Marine Corps Women's Reserve troops sent to Camp Catlin on the Hawaiian island of Oahu, I transported officers to their positions in Pearl Harbor and Honolulu. The motor transport building I worked in backed up to the Navy barracks. One night in early 1945, we heard loud music coming from the other side of the 6-foot chain-link fence that separated us. To our delight, we discovered that actor Jackie Cooper (below) was playing the drums among a group of sailors! The rules that barred us from crossing the fence didn't keep us from enjoying several nights of music and conversation through the chain links.

Within a few months, President Roosevelt passed away and Japan surrendered. By December, I was back in the States—but with a musical memory I'd never forget.

LYLA SPELBRING HOWELL, MI

SMILE! YOU'RE ON KHAKI CAMERA

From 1942 to '45, my 68th Field Evacuation Hospital unit moved from Africa to Italy and then on to France and Germany, following the action so that we could treat the wounded troops. Many wonderful performers treated us to great entertainment along the way. It was in Palermo and Anzio, Italy, in 1943-'44 that we 300-plus soldiers, nurses and officers saw stars like Martha Raye (left and center) and Bob Hope and Frances Langford (right), who often put themselves in harm's way to entertain us. When I was off duty from my X-ray technician job, I had my 4x5 Speed Graphic camera at the ready. I was nicknamed "Jiffy" because I developed my pictures so quickly!

BOB SPRING BELLINGHAM, WA

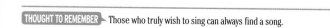

THE HILLS WERE ALIVE "I was with the 45th Infantry Division in Korea in May 1955 when a USO show came to camp," writes Ralph De Baise of Pompano Beach, Florida. "All the entertainers were from the Philippines. There were no seats, so the soldiers found spots on the hillsides. We surely appreciated those entertainers."

THOUGHT TO REMEMBER Those who truly wish to sing can always find a song.

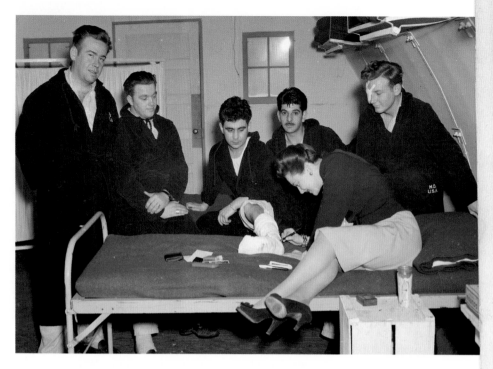

▲ CAST PARTY

"That's Olivia de Havilland, signing the cast of a GI during World War II," says Harold J. Conner of Cincinnati, Ohio. "She came to our island of Shemya, part of the Aleutian chain west of Alaska, to visit GIs hurt in the Battle of Attu. She talked with them about home and even ate with them in the mess hall."

TRIPLE-DECKER FAMILY ▶

"During World War II, I was stationed in San Diego and living off the base with my wife, Frances," writes Don Luther of Warren, Michigan. "Since we were both trained acrobats, we performed many times at various bases in the area. This photograph shows us performing a 'three-high' in the yard with my wife in the middle and our 1-year-old daughter, Darleen, perched on her shoulders."

PX(9-3-42) ADA LENARD'S BAND

▲ **BAND CAMP**

"Since my father, Morton Robbins, was in an Army band during World War II, I'd always assumed that this was a picture taken with a WAC band," says Leslie Robbins of Downers Grove, Illinois. "Through research, I discovered that Ada Leonard had a popular all-female civilian band, the All-American Girl Orchestra, in that era. Ms. Leonard is the glamorous driver of the jeep. Dad is the GI with the big smile to the left of the jeep's front-seat passenger."

Our Heroes
THEIR METTLE STOOD THE TEST

DADDY'S HOME

During the late summer of 1945, I lived in a close-knit neighborhood in Scranton, Pennsylvania. Many of the houses on my street were old and in dire need of repair because the able-bodied men were at war. Families often didn't tell young children—like me—about their fathers because no one could be sure they would come home.

One sunny day, I was sitting on the steps of the grocery store across the street from my house, licking a Sugar Daddy lollipop that the storeowner had given to me. She was very kind and often brought food to the house for my mother, my sister and me.

I had never seen a soldier in person and was surprised when I saw a man in uniform coming down the other side of the street. He was tall, lean, sharply dressed and focused on his destination. When he got to the front of my house, he stopped and walked up onto the porch. He removed his garrison cap and stood staring at the door for a while.

Not knowing what to do, I ran into the store to tell the owner that a soldier was on my front porch. I will never forget the way she got down on both knees, hugged me hard and, with tears on her cheeks, said, "That is your daddy. He came home."

It took a long time to get to know that soldier, but we bonded that summer as we sat together on the front porch, saluting other men in uniform as they passed by on their way home.

JACK HEALEY WESTERLY, RI

HAPPY RETURN Father Joe, 29, and son Jack, 5, are reunited outside their family home. Joe served with the 22nd Field Artillery Battalion during World War II.

HIGH ART Navy flier Howard Miner (left) served among the daring Black Cats during World War II. While resting at base camp between missions, he designed his flight squadron's logo (below) and painted it on many a fellow pilot's jacket.

ONE COOL CAT

I followed Dad through our basement to his file cabinet. He pulled out a large folder filled with sheets of worn manila paper. I was about 5 then, in the mid-1950s, and that was the first time I saw his sketches—exciting images of planes, jungles and soldiers. I was so proud of those drawings that I often snuck down to the basement with friends to show off Dad's art. Then one day, the cabinet was locked.

When Dad passed away in 2011, my family discovered several boxes of writing and artwork saved from his military days. I was relieved to find the sketches but wasn't expecting the wealth

of photographs and journals. For months, I sorted through Dad's things and edited his writings to share his life story in the book *Sketches of a Black Cat*, released on Veterans Day 2012.

My dad, Howard Miner, was a Black Cat, part of a Navy squadron that flew at night without lights in lumbering PBY Catalina amphibious aircraft. The Cats prowled the skies, making light bombing runs, providing reliable reconnaissance and raising havoc with enemy ships. The squadron operated out of the limelight, and their missions were long, frequently 10 to 12 hours. Back at "Black Cat camp," Dad found himself drawing and

writing about his experiences.

Sketches of a Black Cat follows his extraordinary journey through training and two tours in the South Pacific. Since the book came out, former Black Cats have contacted me, some from Dad's own squadron. His art has been displayed at the Evergreen Aviation & Space Museum in McMinnville, Oregon, and the National Museum of the Pacific War in Fredericksburg, Texas.

I feel so fortunate to be taking Dad's story and artwork on the road. It's been quite an adventure, and I'm forever grateful for Dad, the Cats and all the "average guys" of our greatest generation.

RON MINER SALEM, OR

THOUGHT TO REMEMBER ➤ Courage is the mastery of fear.

RAPID-FIRE BABY BOOM ➤

"That's me and my son (back row, middle) with five other servicemen and their firstborns," says Charlie Gattuso, Roanoke, Virginia. "The babies were born at our Marine Corps air station at a cost of $8.75 each. Our families all became close friends."

◄ AN EMOTIONAL RIDE

Jack Gutstein—an Army radioman stationed in New Delhi, India, during World War II—was also an amateur photographer, snapping photos that later became award winners. His daughter, Carla Brooke from Palm Coast, Florida, shared this one Jack took in 1945, when he was one of 700 GIs on board the *USS General Bliss*, passing the time in peaceful waters on their way back home.

"How many men does it take to create a human Liberty Bell? Photographers Arthur S. Mole and John D. Thomas found that it was about 25,000 soldiers when they took this picture at Fort Dix, New Jersey, in 1918."

RENEE GERLACH PHOENIX, AZ

MODEL MARINE "After an honorable discharge from the Marine Corps in 1953, I went to college in Milwaukee and joined the Marine Corps Reserve Unit," writes Pat Mahoney (left) of Green Bay, Wisconsin. "While attending a landing craft exercise in Newport News, Virginia, I was one of four men selected for a 'special assignment,' which usually entailed a work duty. Instead, we were taken to a hotel pool, where we took part in a photo shoot to promote the Marine Corps Reserve—complete with pretty girls."

NOW SHOWING If you recall the fun of Saturday matinees, this late-'20s theater lobby in New York City may spark some golden memories of the silver screen. Elaine Wojenski of Burlington, New Jersey, certainly remembers. "The fun started in the ticket line," she writes. "Clutching our 11-cent admission tightly, we said hello to friends. When the lights dimmed, that solemn voice of the newsreel competed with some noisy kids!"

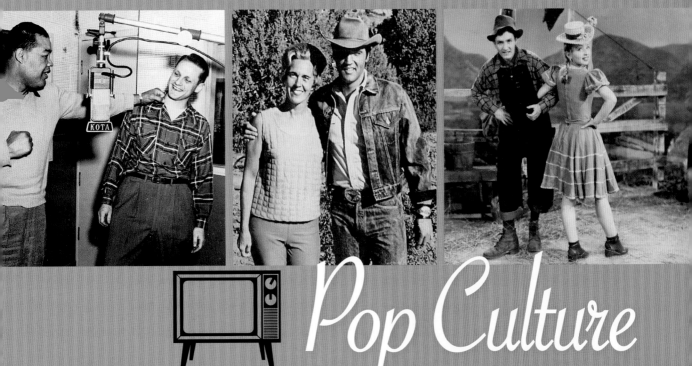

CHAPTER 8

Pop Culture

READY FOR A POP QUIZ? HOW MANY FAB
FADS AND FASHIONS DID YOU FOLLOW... AND
WHICH SHINING STARS OF
MUSIC, MOVIE AND TV FAME RANKED
ON YOUR OWN PERSONAL HIT PARADE?

Screen Stars
LIGHTS...CAMERA...ACTION!

OUR SHIP'S SWEETHEART

Shortly after the Korean War ended, the Navy ship *USS Bennington* suffered a mortal injury in an accidental peacetime blast off the coast of Rhode Island, resulting in the loss of 103 sailors. After the tragedy, the ship was moved to Brooklyn Navy Yard in New York for repairs.

Almost a year later, the *Bennington* was fixed, modernized and scheduled to go back to active duty. The Navy picked me to serve as the *USS Bennington*'s public relations man. On March 31, 1955, I attended a party in the Grand Ballroom of the Astor Hotel in New York City to celebrate the ship's restoration.

Several of the officers and enlisted men learned that Marilyn Monroe was in the city promoting her new movie, *The Seven Year Itch*. They decided to invite Marilyn to be our ship's sweetheart. Marilyn accepted our 8 p.m. invitation. But because of her busy schedule, she didn't show up until around 11 p.m.

The ballroom nearly turned into a riot zone when Marilyn walked out onstage wearing a clingy black satin dress with a white ermine cape draped over her shoulders. As sailors rushed the stage, Marilyn's press agent said, "We're getting out of here!"

Backstage, I realized I had my first real public relations crisis on my hands. Here was the world's hottest movie star, and she was going to pop in and right out again. I knew I had to save the night.

"Can we get a picture of you kissing a sailor good night?" I asked Marilyn hopefully.

She looked at me and with that breathy voice and those luscious lips said, "Why, certainly!"

A Marine immediately volunteered to be in the shot.

"OK, but I need a sailor, too!" I shouted. Nobody came forward. Obviously, they were all too in awe of this beautiful blonde to say a word or move a muscle.

"How about you?" Marilyn whispered to me.

"Oh, OK!" I responded in my most professional manner, my voice cracking a bit. The three of us huddled together as the flashbulbs popped. (That's me at top, to the right of Marilyn.) When she departed, she planted a movie star kiss on the Marine's cheek and on mine.

The next day, our picture appeared in the *New York Mirror* with the headline "It's a Sailor's Life and It Ain't Bad." I was quickly promoted to journalist second class and have been doing public relations ever since.

PAUL LAZZARO THE WOODLANDS, TX

SO MANY STARS, SO LITTLE TIME

In May 1966, my husband and I were spending our honeymoon in New Orleans, Louisiana. While sightseeing, we happened across Lassie, the famed television and movie collie, during the filming of a TV episode.

Lassie's trainer was very friendly (he's in the sunglasses with me and Lassie below) and let us take pictures of this beautiful dog.

As we continued our walk, we ran into a group of excited people and were told that Rod Taylor, a popular movie actor, was making a film and would be coming out to sign autographs.

We were thrilled and said, "Wow, first we see Lassie, and now we get to see Rod Taylor!"

A lovely older woman turned to us and politely but urgently asked where we'd seen Lassie.

When we told her, she hurried off, saying, "I can see Rod Taylor anytime, but I'll never get another chance to see Lassie!"

We still chuckle over that dear lady who preferred to see a dog instead of a handsome movie star.
BETTE VAN WHITE CLOUD, MI

"… SUDDENLY TAB HUNTER WAS KISSING ME!"

It was summer 1955 when a headline in *Screen Album* magazine caught my eye: "Tell Us Why You'd Like to Meet a Star and Win a Trip to Hollywood." I knew who the star of my entry would be. It was my latest heartthrob, Tab Hunter, and I described him in the required 50 words or less.

To my amazement, from 25,000 entries, I won! On New Year's Eve, my mother and I left our St. Louis home and flew to Los Angeles. We were treated like royalty right from the start and even had 50-yard-line tickets for the Rose Bowl.

Early on in our dream week, we toured Hollywood and saw all the things an out-of-towner wants to see. Then we went to Grauman's Chinese Theatre in Hollywood.

When we got back to our hotel, Carl Schroeder, one of *Screen Album*'s managers, asked if I'd like to meet a few stars my own age. Who wouldn't? He clapped his hands and in walked Natalie Wood, Nick Adams and Dennis Hopper! We all had dinner at the Knickerbocker and then went to Natalie's house to play records. (That's Nick, Natalie, me and Dennis, above.)

Friday brought my dream date with Tab Hunter. We met at Warner Brothers in the morning, driving around in a prop car to see where various movies were being made and visiting prop rooms.

That evening, Tab and I had our dinner date at the Mocambo nightclub, where we even danced and met other stars. My dear mother was as thrilled as I was! Our gracious movie star was kind and easy to talk to, and our date ended with a kiss on my cheek and one for my mother.

All too soon, the week was over and I returned to the everyday reality of life in St. Louis. But my adventure wasn't over yet. In November 2005, I happened to see that Tab Hunter was coming to St. Louis for a book signing, so I went to the event with a couple of my friends and my husband. Tab loved the pictures I'd brought along, and I told him that the 50th anniversary of our date was coming in a couple of months. He recalled the time fondly because he had been just getting started in the movies and was treated well as a Hollywood newcomer. He was just as gracious that night as he had been when I was a starry-eyed teen.
JO-ANN COX BUNTON BALLWIN, MO

THOUGHT TO REMEMBER Beauty may fade; good nature never does.

ALL RIGHT, LET'S CONCENTRATE

I spent Sunday, Aug. 24, 1958, pacing the floor at the NBC-TV studios in New York City. I was the producer of a new show called *Concentration* that was going on the air in hours and our key prop, a huge electronic game board, was downstairs, unable to be squeezed into the freight elevator.

Eventually the whole mess miraculously fell into place, and we got the show on the air. Everyone agreed it seemed good enough to last at least 13 weeks. Well, it lasted 14½ years—up to then, the longest-running daytime game show in television history.

We awarded trips around the world, cars, boats, fur coats and diamonds. In all, contestants won $10 million in cash and prizes based on their ability to solve a rebus-style picture puzzle.

Our home viewers were also rewarded with 22,776 one-minute commercials. Sometimes they were harder to produce than the show, requiring elaborate sets, such as full-size kitchens or portions of supermarkets.

And the sponsors could be demanding. When some tough guys insisted our host, Hugh Downs, eat their Rice-A-Roni on the air, Hugh refused. (That's Hugh on the left in the photo below, next to me and Bob Clayton, the show's final host.) Always honest and aboveboard, Hugh was not to be intimidated. A compromise was reached, and Hugh held up an unopened box and smiled.

Often those commercials saved us when things broke down. We needed those 60 seconds to replace a faulty mic or camera or burned-out bulbs.

As television technology changed, so did our show. In the late '50s, color entered the picture. Then came the advent of videotape. Not only did it give us a second chance to correct a goof, but it allowed us to tape shows ahead of time and actually take vacations!

Still, there was nothing like those days of live TV with its wonderful sense of reality, spontaneity and excitement. We had contestants get so excited, they fainted!

Anything that could go wrong usually did, but we lived with it and enjoyed every minute. And so did the viewers.

NORM BLUMENTHAL
WEST HEMPSTEAD, NY

DISHING ON HOLLYWOOD
"In the 1960s and '70s, my mother, Loretta Brauckmann, worked in Hollywood as a caterer to the stars," writes R.C. Santoro of Coos Bay, Oregon. "She took care of some of the major names, making them breakfast, lunch and dinner on the set when movies and television shows were being filmed. During production, Mom always had her picture taken with her new friends, including (from top) Dean Martin, Cliff Robertson and Elvis Presley—plus many more hungry celebrities. Elvis even called her Mom."

1943

THE FIRST VIDEO STAR

Frances Yasney was a music video star before MTV ever broadcast a signal. At 16, she danced in Soundies, which were three-minute black-and-white musicals that were viewed on a device called a Panoram, a jukebox about the size of a refrigerator with a 16 mm film projector. The short films were produced between the summer of 1940 and the winter of 1946.

War-weary patrons out for some entertainment at bars, nightclubs, poolrooms, restaurants, military bases, hotels and dance halls loved Soundies. They would insert a dime to watch stars such as Duke Ellington, Gene Krupa, Cab Calloway and Nat King Cole's trio, among others, play their latest hits, or attractive youngsters like Frances act out a song's theme.

Back in 1939, Frances (nee Weltsch) was a passionate young dancer who often choreographed her own routines. She and a partner were performing one of them to the music of Mike Riley's Big Band on the dance campus at the New York World's Fair when the campus manager spotted them. He offered the duo $5 a day to perform every few hours to help drum up business.

Later, a scout from Triumph Films signed Frances to dance in Soundies. She was just 16 and beautiful—a Betty Grable look-alike—and giddy after having just married her handsome young man, Alfred Duze.

"Our wages were $50 for each movie," says Frances, recalling those thrilling days. "They also gave us costumes and did our hair and makeup. We felt like millionaires." (That's Frances seated in the front row in the photo above and dancing with a partner, top, right.)

To continue doing what she loved and keep the money rolling in, Frances told producers pretty much anything they wanted to hear. Could she square dance? "Of course, I said yes!" she says, recalling that film's number (barnyard scene at right) as nothing like the actual steps she performed later in life as a semiprofessional square dancer.

"We always said yes. And the producers always just seemed hungry for entertainment—and to get the films made."

Soundies featured the best variety of music available in the 1940s and gave several performers a leg up in the entertainment world. The likes of Doris Day, Yvonne De Carlo, Ricardo Montalban and Walter Liberace had their first-time film experiences in the mini movies.

Soundies began falling out of vogue around 1946, just five years after they premiered. Production halted late that year, with the last Soundies released to Panoram owners in March 1947.

Ironically, Frances has never had the pleasure of watching herself in them. She attributes this to the grueling production schedules, but it's also likely that, at only 16, she was too young to enter establishments where alcohol was sold and Panorams were stationed.

"It was just something I did," Frances says about her singular career. "Dancing is in my blood."
MICHAEL Q. BULLERDICK
CAMPBELL HALL, NY

High Notes

ALL SHOOK UP

Fifty-eight years ago, Elvis Presley almost started a family feud when my husband, Vic, and I went to see the hip-shaking sensation with Vic's sister, Merle, and her husband, Ed, in 1956.

For a whopping $1.50 each, we bought tickets to the King's 9 p.m. performance at the Polk Theatre in Lakeland, Florida. Neither Vic nor Ed wanted to see "that weird guy wiggle his hips in front of a bunch of screeching teenagers." But when Merle and I said, "That's fine, we'll go alone," they both got into the car and grumbled all the way to the concert.

When Elvis finally stepped out from behind the velvet curtain for his 15-minute set, the crowd went wild—except for Vic and Ed, of course. Our party-pooper husbands sat with their arms folded across their chests.

As Elvis started singing his first song, "Don't Be Cruel," the theater erupted into a frenzy of yelling women. Merle and I clapped wildly with the kids, but Ed and Vic snorted and squirmed in their seats, saying, "Let's get out of here!"

During the second song, "Love Me Tender," we could hardly hear Elvis' crooning over the screams. By then, Merle and I were teary-eyed and on our feet, stretching our necks to get a better look at Elvis the Pelvis.

"Sit down and act your age," Ed hissed, pulling Merle's hand. Vic tugged on my shirttail and said something, too, but I just ignored him and watched Elvis.

Elvis struck a pose, ran his hand through his pompadour and announced that the next song would close his show. He thrust the mic forward, leaned into it and cut loose with the leg-jiggling "Hound Dog." The audience responded with yells and claps that lasted well after the King slipped back behind the curtain.

Driving home, Merle and I mimicked Elvis singing "Hound Dog." We laughed so hard the guys couldn't help but join in.

What fun it had been to let down our hair and experience this teen idol in action. Merle and I remained avid Elvis fans long after he died in 1977. How sad that he's no longer with us. Now a white-haired grandmother, I'm unashamed to admit I still love Elvis Presley, the King forever!

BETTY J. VICKERS
ST. GEORGE, UT

HAIL TO THE KING Betty snapped the photo of Elvis signing autographs after his show at the Polk Theatre (right). Married couple Vic and Betty share a loving embrace in front of the camera (above).

STRUMMIN' WITH THE STARS

In 1940, when I was 10 years old, I talked my mother into buying guitars for my brother, Floyd, and me. We learned to play by practicing along with 78 rpm records featuring guitar masters like Jerry Byrd and Little Roy Wiggins. It also helped that we lived in Nashville, America's country music capital.

Soon, Floyd and I started performing in public, and in high school, we formed our own local band. My biggest break came in 1948: Red Foley, the star of the Grand Ole Opry radio show, needed a steel guitar player and, to my amazement, I got the job!

Here I was at 18, backing up a who's who of superstars—Tennessee Ernie Ford, Minnie Pearl, Roy Acuff and Hank Williams—inside the hallowed Ryman Auditorium. Because I was so young, people liked pulling tricks on me. A favorite was secretly untuning my guitar. I wouldn't know it until I started playing!

A highlight for me was traveling to Germany in 1949 with the first Opry performers ever to play in Europe. (I'm the guy in front, second from left, in the shot of our group above.)

My Opry days ended when I got drafted in 1952. Later, I attended art school on the GI Bill and started a second great career as a graphic artist. I was incredibly blessed to be part of the Grand Ole Opry for those four years. And I'm still living my boyhood dream playing at steel guitar venues around the country.

BILLY ROBINSON GALLATIN, TN

▲ BIG HAIR AND SPARKLY PANTS

"As a member (far left) of Abbie Neal and the Ranch Girls in the 1960s, I performed all across Nevada and on the *Beachcombers* entertainment ship in Kodiak, Alaska," says Lucille Werner, whose stage name was Lucille Carr. "I'm still playing guitar and singing, and I do 11 different yodel songs."

THOUGHT TO REMEMBER ➤ The hardest instrument to play gracefully is second fiddle.

Kidding Around

Saturday morning cartoons, Disney movies and larger-than-life TV heroes were like catnip to kiddies at a time when having fun was as simple as child's play.

▲ KANGAROO COURT

"In 1957, our children (from left) Suzann, Russell and Kathy were watching their favorite television program, *Captain Kangaroo*, when we lived in Roy, Utah," write Charles and Jean Parker, who now reside in Layton. "After this photo was taken, we had three more children. Since then, the kids have all married and raised their own families, and we are blessed with numerous grandchildren and great-grandchildren."

▲ BACKSTAGE WITH BOZO

"Meeting Bozo the Clown and his co-stars thrilled my daughters Kristi and Karen in 1969," says David Burnett, Naples, Florida. "After applying for tickets, it took three years before we got to attend the show. Our fan club included Kristi, two neighbor pals and Karen."

➤ HAPPY TRAILS TO YOUTH

"In 1952, I entered a coloring contest sponsored by *TV Digest*, with 10 lucky winners getting to meet Roy Rogers at Madison Square Garden," says Larry Warfel, Webster, Florida. "I was so excited to be among the winners. We rode on a chartered bus to New York City. I recall talking to Roy Rogers and Dale Evans and meeting Bullet, their German shepherd, in their dressing room, where we had a picture taken (right; I'm at bottom right) and Roy signed all of the winning entries. Then, as *TV Digest* noted, we enjoyed 'the razzle-dazzle of the Roy Rogers Rodeo, with ridin', ropin', bronco bustin' and horse tricks, cotton candy, cowboy hats and souvenirs.'"

"Some people may think 'Disneymania' is a recent phenomenon. But it was in 1951 when my Aunt Camilla bought me (right) and my twin brother, Bruce, these cool Disney character outfits."

BARRY DANIELS SACO, ME

PART OF THE GANG ➤

"On a 1937 trip to the Steel Pier in Atlantic City, New Jersey, my brother Bob Mertz and I, ages 10 and 7, posed with Petey, the dog from the *Our Gang* movies," says Jean Crowell of Medford. "The more laid-back pose (bottom right) belonged to our nephew Harry Burton Jr., who was about 2 or 3 months old. He was the son of my sister Emma, who was 17 years older than I was. We lived in Gloucester back then and enjoyed the many attractions along the Atlantic City Boardwalk."

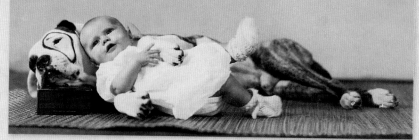

THOUGHT TO REMEMBER ➤ It's nice to be important, but it's more important to be nice.

POP CULTURE   **161**

Brushes With Fame

GOOD LUCK FOR THE STARSTRUCK

TARZAN MADE A SPLASH IN RHODE ISLAND POOL

I had just stepped onto the starting block for the last leg of our 200-yard freestyle relay when a voice behind me said, "Good luck, son." It sent a chill up my spine because the voice belonged to a hero from my youth: Tarzan, also known as Johnny Weissmuller.

It happened in 1950 during my senior year in East High School in Pawtucket, Rhode Island. That year, we had two all-American relay teams, and I swam on both.

Tarzan—he was never Johnny Weissmuller to us—had an aquatics show in Providence. To publicize it, he was invited to the Pawtucket Boys Club to witness our two relays trying to break the local pool record.

On that Sunday, the poolside was filled with kids and their parents, and the small seating area was jammed to capacity.

When Weissmuller came in, cheers rang off the tiled walls. When he let out his Tarzan yell, the noise from the cheering crowd reached record levels.

He then ran over to the diving board and pounced into the pool, breaking the board and splashing some of the crowd, much to their delight.

Tarzan next told the crowd they were going to witness two record-breaking all-American relay teams "attempt to break the pool record of this magnificent club." You would have thought it was an Olympic record, three of which he once held.

We swam the events and broke the record, then Tarzan clasped the hand of each of us as we climbed out of the pool. The local newspaper wanted a photo for the next day's edition. While the other fellows were debating who should drop into the pool, I jumped in. Tarzan was showing me how to stroke, and I look as if I'm saying, "Are you serious?"

The next day, my proud father and mother were taking that crumpled newspaper all over the neighborhood!

Weissmuller spent time after the exhibition talking to us about his Olympic experiences and asking about our families and our future. When he left the club—vacant by then—we heard one last Tarzan call and knew it was for us.

LOU BRIERELY COLUMBIA, SC

A PRESIDENTIAL POSE

During vacation from high school teaching in the summer of 1954, I traveled through the West with my friend Theo.

While at Glacier National Park in Montana, we stopped at the park lodge for a bite to eat. Suddenly, there was an announcement on the PA system that Ronald Reagan was in the area, filming a movie with Barbara Stanwyck, and that he was due at the lodge for a lunch break. When Mr. Reagan arrived, I jumped at the chance to ask him if he'd mind posing for a picture. He graciously consented and stood by his car. That's his son in the front seat.

ROSEMARY TRETTIN APPLETON, WI

I FLEW WITH AMELIA EARHART

In the summer of 1927, I entered a contest offering a free airplane ride to the 10 women who guessed closest to the number of beans in a big hourglass. My wild guess landed me, a farm girl, the ride of my life!

Not only was it my first airplane ride, it was hosted by famous aviatrix Amelia Earhart, who was vice president of Boston-Maine Airways. Amelia was gracious and friendly and I loved every moment of the flight, especially the beautiful Maine countryside.

"Would you like to take a picture of the dam over the Kennebec?" she asked me.

I did, so she asked the pilot to bank the airplane for our photos. I took a pictures of the dam, of our state Capitol dome and of the road leading to our farm 8 miles out of Augusta. Amelia told us that we were 7,000 feet up and traveling at over 55 miles an hour!

For me, seeing the ground from the air was as beautiful as viewing it from a mountaintop. Boston-Maine Airways had been emphasizing its "efficiency," but it seemed to me that "beauty" could be just as powerful an enticement to get people to fly.

After we landed, Amelia posed for a picture with us—a thoughtful gesture at the end of a wonderful, unforgettable afternoon.

JULIA BROWN
SANTA BARBARA, CA

BOXER TAUGHT HIM A LESSON ➤

"In 1938, boxing fans eagerly awaited the rematch between Joe Louis and the German fighter Max Schmeling," says Verne Lotz, Rapid City, South Dakota. "My father told me to tune in the fight on the radio and to call him when it began. Unfortunately, Joe threw a first-round knockout punch, and Dad missed the exciting moment due to my dawdling.

"My timing improved as I pursued a career in radio and TV. In 1953, I interviewed Louis at the radio station where I was working. Luckily, he pulled his punch in this photo!"

▲ MEMORIES OF THE BABE HIT HOME

"My father was a French diplomat, so I attended a private school in Paris," says Larry Lahm, Corvallis, Oregon. "In 1935, when I was 15, Babe Ruth was on a pleasure trip and visited our school. We gathered on the softball field and, since I was the pitcher, the headmaster called my name. When I faced the 'Sultan of Swat,' I was nervous as I tried to put the pitches over the imaginary plate. He didn't miss one! He took such terrific swings that he'd turn completely around. It was unbelievable how hard he hit the ball. The Babe also gave me some batting tips, and a click of the camera caught this photo."

CHILD-BEARING PRESIDENT

I was orphaned as a young child, and my siblings and I went to live with an uncle. When my oldest brother married in 1927 at age 21, he took all his younger siblings back home.

About this same time, President Calvin Coolidge and his wife were scheduled to make a stop in our town of Hammond, Indiana, to dedicate Wicker Memorial Park to the World War I veterans. Someone decided that a little girl should present flowers to Mrs. Coolidge to help make the presidential couple feel welcome. I was picked to be the girl.

As you can see in the photo, the first lady is holding her flowers as the president holds 6-year-old me. The photograph is now in the Library of Congress.

I think the city was smart to choose an orphan to present the flowers, because no one could complain too loudly that his or her child wasn't picked. And I wonder if Sister Loretta, the principal at my school, was biased, choosing me over my sisters Helen, Lottie and Tillie!

LORETTA JABLONSKI KRZYMINSKI
GREENFIELD, WI

◄ OUR MOMENT WITH JOHN GLENN

"In 1962, astronaut John Glenn orbited the Earth and captured the hearts of the American people," writes Jackie Fisher of Somerset, Ohio. "A few years later, he attended a football game at Sheridan High School. My husband, Richard Fisher, was principal of the high school at that time and was fortunate enough to have his picture taken with Glenn. My son, Doug Fisher, is also in the photo. They couldn't stop smiling."

THOUGHT TO REMEMBER ~ People who know the joy of receiving a compliment, compliment others easily.

POP CULTURE 165

Fads We Loved

Bobby socks, mop-top haircuts, miniskirts and go-go boots: Oh, to what lengths we would go to be on the cutting edge of the latest fads and fashion crazes.

HANGIN' AROUND "It was a typical afternoon during our high school days in 1953 when this photo was taken," says Ramona Larson, Hettinger, North Dakota. "I'm between my friends Bert Nelson (left) and Rosella Lillehaug. We had on pedal pushers, saddle shoes, bobby socks and white button-front shirts. To be that young again would be wonderful. When I look at this picture, I am!"

BEATLE WANNABE "Here I am in 1966, sitting on my 1958 Chevy and sporting a Beatle haircut, which the girls seemed to like," writes Bob Gouveia of Burlington, Massachusetts. "Many boys also had the Beatle boots I'm wearing—I had about four different styles. I even saw the Beatles in concert—$5 for admission. My dad said we teenagers looked as if we came from another planet. He took photos so that when we got older, we could see how ridiculous we looked. 'Stamp it out before it multiplies!' he'd joke."

A BALLOONING FAD "My daughters Kathy and Connie had a blast in 1971 with the Super Elastic Bubble Plastic they got for Christmas," says JoAnn Schueller Cooke, Reseda, California. "The toy, made by Wham-O, came in a metal tube and included a plastic straw. You squeezed plastic from the tube onto the end of the straw and blew to see how big a bubble you could make."

THOUGHT TO REMEMBER ➤ The best way to forget other troubles is to wear tight shoes.

MINI WAS MAJOR NEWS The enduring miniskirt made its debut in 1966 and continues to bob in and out of fashion. Mary Felician of Wind Lake, Wisconsin, shared this photo of herself with her future husband, Jerry, at a dance in the late '60s. "I loved miniskirts," she says, "especially after 12 years of Catholic school and having to wear long woolen skirts that went down to my ankles. I felt like a real rebel!"

MOM WILL LOVE 'EM "Flowers were front and center in this photo taken May 10, 1958, by my father, Tom Gandolfo," says Pauline Bowyer of Caledonia, Illinois. "I don't know who the woman was, but the storefront was S.S. Kresge in the Bronx, New York. Dad was an assistant manager there at the time and later became general store manager. In addition to the potted plants, assorted items inside the window presented as possible Mother's Day gifts included handbags and packaged blouses. The food advertisements invited customers in for soda fountain treats like a pineapple sundae, a hamburger plus Coke, and Kresge's hot coffee."

CHAPTER 9

Holiday Spirit

SHUTTERBUGS ARE HAPPIEST WHEN THEY'RE
CAPTURING THE MAGIC OF A HOLIDAY,
BIRTHDAY OR CONFETTI-WORTHY OCCASION.
SO LET THE CELEBRATIONS BEGIN!

Celebrating a New Year

CHAMPAGNE AND BIRTHDAY CAKES

CAN YOU TOP THIS?

For my 10th birthday in 1953, I had a "tacky party." Only one photo was taken at the big event (left).

Photography was an extravagance my father didn't cotton to. When a roll of film was developed, into the album went one shot each of our car, visiting relatives, Easter, Thanksgiving, Christmas and Jeep, our parakeet.

More recently, I told my 80-year-old uncle about my granddaughter's birthday party, a spectacular affair where you wouldn't have batted an eye if The Flying Wallendas had swooped in.

"I had a birthday party once," my uncle said. "Two friends came over after school. We ate watermelon and were allowed to spit the seeds in the yard."

DONNA MULLINAX BROWN
VILLA RICA, GA

HAPPY TO LOOK LIKE HOPPY

Back in 1950, all kids wanted to look like their hero, Hopalong Cassidy. That was certainly the case with my brother, John "Ron" Ravano.

Hoppy outfits were available for kids, but our parents, John and Helen, couldn't afford the complete wardrobe. So they asked relatives to each buy a piece for Ronnie's seventh birthday. You can imagine my brother's surprise and excitement as he opened each package and came closer to being able to look like his hero.

From that day on, it was hard to get Ronnie to wear anything else. He was the envy of the neighborhood.

Even today, when my brother looks at this photo of him with our parents (right), he says, "I wish I still had that outfit."

RICHARD RAVANO CAMERON PARK, CA

HAPPY BIRTHDAY, MOM "Fiesta Dinnerware was all the go in the '50s," says John Spangler of Hanover, Pennsylvania. "On my wife Mae's birthday in April 1954, she received a Fiesta ware cup and saucer to complete her set. This slide of Mae, me and our daughters, Sandy and Janice, was taken in the kitchen of our home in East Greenville, Pennsylvania." The colorful collectible dishes made a comeback in 1986 after a 13-year retirement.

HER BEST PRESENT EVER "I was born in 1943 on my mom's birthday, Oct. 10," writes John Wehrman of Green Bay, Wisconsin. "A local newspaper ran this photo of my mother, Ruth, and me when I turned 2 and she turned 24."

CONFETTIED KIDS "On New Year's Day 1961, two of our children, Stanley (left) and Sally, offered to help clean up the living room after a New Year's Eve party," says Harry Sheppard from San Mateo, California. "The kids decided to have their own New Year's party by draping themselves with confetti."

THOUGHT TO REMEMBER → You have to get older, but you don't have to grow up.

▲ **FELIZ ANO NUEVO!** "Prohibition was in effect in 1925, so my aunt and uncle (middle couple) took a Caribbean cruise with friends and celebrated New Year's Eve in Havana Harbor," writes Betty Davidson from Stuart, Florida.

HE'LL GROW INTO IT ▶
"When our son, Donald, was 2, my husband got the bright idea of making him the New Year's baby for 1943," says Beatrice Allen of Bellows Falls, Vermont. "He made the banner, then put his big hat on Donald. We thought the photo was so cute."

▲ **RAISE A GLASS**
"My sons Jerry and Roger toasted the New Year with Kool-Aid on Dec. 31, 1957, at our home in Omaha, Nebraska," writes Hazel Magner from Omaha.

◀ **YABBA DABBA DOO!**
Fred and Barney from *The Flintstones* were among guests at Danny Smith's sixth birthday party in 1970. "Then, parties were simple, with a few neighborhood kids, cake or cupcakes and pin the tail on the donkey," says Danny's mom, Angela of Wantagh, New York.

▲ **IN SEVENTH HEAVEN**
"With eight children, we economized by throwing a big birthday party for each child when he or she turned 7," says Phyllis Glanzman, Mondovi, Wisconsin. "In this 1959 photo, Shelley holds a cake I made shaped like a bassinet, with a doll tucked into it."

Heartwarming Holidays

REMEMBERING THE ONES WE LOVE

REAL A-PEEL
Alvin's mother, Reba, treasured the gift she received on Mother's Day in 1938. She's pictured at left with Alvin's father, Sam, and their youngest son, Daniel, several years after the Great Depression.

THE PERFECT GIFT

"Use this to buy your mother a gift for Mother's Day," my dad said as he handed me a dime.

It was 1938, and I was 10 years old. Being the older of two boys, I took the mission seriously.

Woolworth's five-and-dime was the place to shop if you had only a dime to spend. It was while looking in the kitchen hardware section that I spotted what I thought was the perfect gift: a double-bladed, swivel-handled potato peeler. It would be so much better than Mom's old paring knife.

On Mother's Day, Mom opened her present. I studied her eyes and saw only delight as she exclaimed, "What a nice gift! Oh, thank you!" She kissed my brother and me on the forehead.

I was eager to see the new peeler in operation, but I noticed that my mother kept using her old paring knife. After several days of disappointment, I finally asked her, "Mom, why don't you use the new potato peeler?"

Taking a deep breath, she decided to level with me.

"Alvin, the best part of the potato is just under the skin,"

she explained. "This new type of peeler wastes too much of the potato and removes the best part." Seeing my hurt look, she added, "I'll keep it in the drawer forever to remind me what a wonderful Mother's Day it was."

Fifty years later, my brother and I stood in the same kitchen, sorting through Mom and Dad's estate. I spotted the double-bladed, swivel-handled potato peeler. I picked it up, wondering how many times she held it in her hands and thought, *What a wonderful Mother's Day it was.*

ALVIN ROSSER SPARTA, NJ

HAVE A CIGAR, DADS!

According to a *Milwaukee Sentinel* newspaper article dated June 17, 1947, 25 babies were born two days earlier, on Father's Day, in various hospitals around Milwaukee, Wisconsin.

Seventeen of the fathers were able to come in for this photo. We were at the Elks Club in Milwaukee, where John A.

Seramur (far right) presented all of the new fathers with cigars. This exemplified the start of the baby boom generation.

The man at far left in back was cropped out of the newspaper photo. The other men in the back row, from left, are Robert Schrieber, Albert J. Ehlenfeldt, Richard Grudzielanek, Russell L. Harmeyer, LeRoy Stewart, Joe Feilen and John Harrington.

The men in front, from left, are Russell W. Bowmann, Donald Brock, Clarence T. Huebschman, Raymond Moon, me, Leonard Rubner, Joseph Pekrul, Harvey Scherr and Lloyd Davis.

The kids from that year would now be turning 68. Our daughter is a grandmother.

HANS FAISS RUSSELLVILLE, AL

CHIC CHAPEAU "Smiling on Mother's Day 1962 was Marie Antoinette Michand, mom of my friend Helen St. Onge," says Jane Crocker, Elizabeth City, North Carolina. "Helen and her husband, Vin, were very close to my husband, Bill, and me."

MADE WITH LOVE "Mary Jacqueline, Judy and Don Jr. were gazing upon a heart-shaped cake I baked for Valentine's Day in 1965," writes mom Shirley Bardella, Willcox, Arizona.

COLD HANDS...WARM HEART "This was my special valentine to Grandma in 1931, when I was 13," writes Doris Tonry of Elyria, Ohio. "The snow was crusty, and after several tries, I managed to dig out a big frozen valentine heart for her."

FRONT-PAGE NEWS "I treasure this photo of my mother, Harriet McCulloch, my sister, Kathryn, and my brother, Timothy," says Laurel Graham of Warsaw, Indiana. "A friend of my father's took this picture on Mother's Day 1942 for the front page of the *Saginaw News* in Michigan. I feel it captures the essence of the times."

VALENTINE VITTLES Joanne Shumaker of Swanton, Ohio, who got this slide at a rummage sale, later discovered it was a 1961 photograph of a Valentine's Day party enjoyed by hearing-impaired classmates at Hardley School in Saginaw, Michigan.

REMEMBERING DAD ON FATHER'S DAY

A butcher, a baker, a candlestick maker: Those are about the only jobs my dad never tried.

If it was broke, Mike Tuohy could fix it. If it wasn't broke, he'd fiddle with it until it was—and then, boy, could he fix it.

Dad was born in 1915 and learned early to be creative, economical and inquisitive. We often heard the story of how he put a brick on a board and jumped on the other end to see what would happen—and was rewarded with a dented head!

After graduating from St. Rita High School on Chicago's South Side, he worked as a stevedore. The hours were long and hard, but Dad made a living for his wife and five kids.

Occasionally, he brought things home from the docks, such as the baby lamb he'd saved from slaughter. We kept it in the kitchen of our small bungalow until our cousins gave it a home at their place in the country, saving Mom's sanity.

In the early 1950s, Dad discovered television. Through a correspondence course, he learned how television sets worked and built up a fantastic repair business.

"If your TV gets screwy, call Tuohy" was his motto. He fixed TVs until the day before he died.

Also during the '50s, Dad dug a hole and started a basement. And if building a room when he was 40 wasn't enough, he built another at age 64. What a guy! He was strong, hardworking, creative, kind and loving.

After Mom died in 1968, Dad lived alone for 15 years, but not "lonely" alone. My brother Bob and sister Elaine lived with him most of that time.

Then one day, a small notice in the newspaper's personals column caught his eye: "65, nice looking, would like to

meet a compatible partner for companionship and friendship."

Four months later, in 1983, Dad and Janet Kurtzweil were married. In their 13 years together, they shared a lot. Travel was always high on their list.

They went everywhere, but not by plane. Dad didn't like to fly and often said, "If God wanted me to fly, he'd have put feathers on my back." To prove his point, Dad once offered to drive to Hawaii.

Dad always did things his way. He was a fixer of our house and knew how to repair anything… his way. He also was a fixer of the family. He taught us how to be family. And, he was a fixer of

himself. He didn't follow doctors' rules. He survived 81 years on Michael Tuohy's rules—and when he couldn't fix himself anymore, he got to work fixing his exit.

He chose to stay at home and told the professionals "no more." He kept family around. He went to bed. My dad woke up with feathers on his back and he's not afraid to fly anymore.

He fixed it for his eternity.

Godspeed, Dad.

JANET TUOHY TERRA
OAK LAWN, IL

THOUGHT TO REMEMBER → The best gifts are tied with heartstrings…yours.

Easter Blessings

IT'S A SPRING EGGSTRAVAGANZA

THE EASTER BASKET

I've lived in Lorain, Ohio, all my life, and I've had my picture taken in front of the larger-than-lifesize Easter basket in Lakeview Park for as long as I can remember.

Though Lake Erie, which the park borders, is a wonderful place to swim in the summer, the Easter basket takes center stage in the spring.

A park employee named David Shukait built the novelty, finishing it in 1941. It stands about 7 feet high, 10 feet wide and 5 feet deep. Every Easter, park employees fill it with giant colored eggs.

According to a story in the *Cleveland Plain Dealer*, David knew a little bit about boat building and applied those principles to the Easter basket. He used curved wood and iron and molded wet concrete to them. The statue came together one layer at a time.

The basket was such a novelty that it quickly became a local attraction and holiday tradition. People come from all over to have family pictures taken there at Easter. When I was a child, there was a wire basket of real bunnies in front of the landmark, which was so exciting!

I often look back at our Easter photos and marvel at how I've grown over the years from a child to a teen to a young mother in 1963 (in the yellow coat and hat with my daughter, Pamela, at right) and a grandmother in 2009 (top).

The real Easter bunnies are no longer there, but I still visit the basket with my three children and six grandchildren.

PATRICIA SUTORUS WASH LORAIN, OH

HARD TO HIDE This huge Easter basket, built from wood, iron and concrete, has become an Ohio landmark and the setting for generations of family snaps.

SHEEPISH MODEL ➤
"Our pet lamb, Tinkerbell, was always willing to play dress-up with my sisters and me," writes Toddi Darlington of Thermopolis, Wyoming. "Teri (right), Jaci (middle) and I made her wear this ensemble—complete with a baby blue beret—in 1964."

IN THEIR EASTER HATS "Getting new duds for Easter was a tradition for our sons (from left), Tim, Dave and Charlie," says Pat Stenner of Plain City, Ohio. "This year, 1958, Dave's basket had a toy airplane tucked in with the candy and colored eggs. Two of the boys went on to be pilots and one became an air traffic controller."

"My fiance, Ed, and I were dressed to the nines for church on Easter 1958 in Culver City, California. My mother, Alice, made my dress and even hand-sewed the polka dots to my white gloves to match."

DOROTHY BORLAND ENCINO, CA

THOUGHT TO REMEMBER Of all the things you wear, your expression is the most important.

Parading Around Town

SOMETHING TO STRUT ABOUT

GIRLS BANDED TOGETHER

Columbus Day was reason enough for a parade in Yonkers, New York, back in 1939.

The band was from Commerce High School, an experimental commercial school that trained students for employment in the business world.

The band had 225 marchers, all girls, and the school had approximately 1,200 students. When I was accepted to the school along with 80 or so other boys, we discovered that boys were outnumbered by girls by about 3 to 1. I thought I'd died and gone to heaven. Eventually, one of those girls became my wife.

An amateur photographer at the time, I crawled up on a store roof to get this shot with my Speed Graflex, and it's fun to see the details that I captured, such as license plates and store signs. My darkroom was in the cellar at home, between the coal bin and the furnace. The dust problem was a nightmare!

ALFRED LA VORGNA HICKSVILLE, NY

QUEEN OF THE MAY "My grandmother, then 16, was standing on an automobile underneath her giant hoop skirt in this parade in 1917," says Cathy Rozman of Plymouth, Michigan.

SHE SCORED A HIT Apple Queen Lee Ettinger (at far left on float with her court) thought tossing an apple to the judges of a 1961 parade would impress them. Unintentionally, her flying fruit ended up bonking an unsuspecting judge on his bald head. "Our float didn't win any prizes," Lee writes from St. Johns, Michigan.

PARADING PRINCESSES "Here I am (right), lining up for the annual Auburn Days parade in 1954," says Gayle Kroke of Auburn, Washington. "Mom decorated my trike with flowers. My friend Betty Jo Ewing is in front of me in her dance costume."

TORCHBEARER "My family had just moved to King George, Virginia, in 1965," writes Suzanne Bevan, Fredericksburg. "Everyone was friendly, so when someone asked me to be on a float in a local parade, I accepted. I ended up being the only one on it–and covered with gray eye shadow to boot!"

Halloween Pranks & Giving Thanks

There's no denying the beauty of autumn—from costumed kids collecting candy to grateful families counting their blessings. It's a season for bountiful photos, suitable for framing.

▲ MASTERS OF DISGUISE

The trick to trick-or-treating for Steve and Dave Gunderson (above in the 1950s) was finding bags big enough. "Sometimes they used pillowcases," says mom Annie Rue, Everett, Washington. "The boys always came home with lots of treats. It was work, too—our neighborhood was fairly rural, so they did plenty of walking. Occasionally, we parents tagged along with the boys. Afterward, we'd have the neighborhood kids over for a party and bobbing for apples." Despite the big sacks, there were no tummy aches, Annie adds. "We doled out the treats to them a little at a time so they didn't overeat."

▲ A MEDLEY OF MUGS

The Thompson family carved out time for plenty of Halloween fun in the 1960s. "This slide was taken at Pica-Boo Campground in East Troy, Wisconsin," write Bruce and Joyce Thompson of Waukesha, Wisconsin. Joyce is seated with her children (from left), Steve, Robin, Mark and Ann, and a half-dozen friendly faces set to brighten their autumn doorstep.

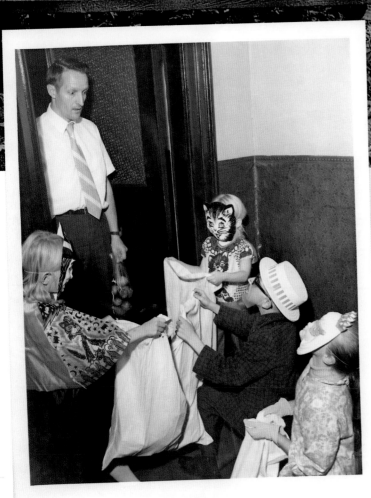

◄ TOO CUTE TO SPOOK

Surprised dad Royden Hunter prepares to treat his four little monsters to fresh apples on Halloween night. Thank you, Nina McLean, for sharing this far-from-frightening family photo from 1970.

◀ NO SCAREDY-CATS

Superstition held little weight with their black-cat-loving daughters Glenda (left) and Donna in 1963, say Don and Avis Henderson from Prescott, Arizona. The grinning jack-o'-lantern looks unphased by the inky felines, too.

▲ TURKEY MIGRATION

"In the late 1950s, I got the crazy idea to move my family from Nebraska to Oregon—which seemed like the Wild West back then," Phil Snyder told his daughter, Marcia Petrick of Hillsboro, Oregon. "We couldn't afford moving vans, so my wife loaded our four kids (above) and our possessions into our station wagon, and I followed them in our farm truck, packed with everything else. I'd raised turkeys in Nebraska, so I bought a turkey ranch in the Willamette Valley, south of Portland. We raised about 20,000 birds a year. In 1960, I bought 20 acres overlooking the valley and built a four-bedroom house—all for $20,000! I'm thankful for our pioneering spirit. Success begins with an idea and a zest for life."

THOUGHT TO REMEMBER ~ Gratitude is always the right attitude.

CLOWN FACES ➤
"These two happy clowns who surprised me on Halloween 1979 are my grandsons Matthew and Eric Redden, ages 7 and 5, respectively," says B.J. Redden of Holyoke, Massachusetts. "As you can see, Matt got into the Halloween spirit by losing a couple of teeth right before the holiday."

◀ **STRANGE COMPANIONS**
A seafaring bandit, a bloodsucking ghoul and a cowpoke were ready to head out in search of Halloween loot in Cleveland, Ohio, in 1956. "I'm the vampire in the middle, my brother Terry is the pirate and our cousin Jeff Alexander is the cowboy," says Ron Holley of Chandler, Arizona. "We were sometimes disappointed we couldn't wear more than the masks when the weather got too cold."

▲ EAGER EATERS

"In this shot, Janet and Craig Hutchens, my niece and nephew, were ready to sit down to Thanksgiving dinner at their Aunt Bea's house in Renton, Washington," says Beatrice Bard of Enumclaw. Check out those 1960s drapes and that knotty pine kitchen paneling.

◄ A HAM WITH TURKEY

"On my son Mike's first Thanksgiving, in 1955, he was hamming it up with his drumstick while his cousin, a month older, kept shying away from the camera," writes Lucille Duh, who has remained in the same ranch-style house in Piscataway, New Jersey.

Lights All Aglow

REKINDLING HOLIDAY JOYS

HANUKKAH HEROINE
The author smiles on her confirmation day in 1973 with parents Milton and Alita Canis.

FLAMING OUT TO THE HANUKKAH STOMP

It was Hanukkah 1972, and my Sunday school class was selected to light the giant 5-foot menorah on the platform at Temple Israel in St. Louis. The sisterhood had decided to make the menorah look extra special that year by putting heavy gold toppers on each candlestick.

I was chosen to hold the shamus (or helper candle). Each child would come up to me, light her candle and place the candle in the menorah. I was to place the final candle on top. Of course at age 15, we couldn't help but suppress giggles as each classmate came up.

It was my big moment. Time to put the last candle on. But all those candles, plus the weight of the new gold toppers, were just too much for the menorah. The whole thing toppled forward and candles fell onto the carpet, igniting small fires.

All my friends scattered, leaving me alone on the platform. I valiantly began to stomp the fires out. The rabbi came down from the pulpit above, lifted his long black robe up to his shins and began stomping with me.

I don't know what horrified me more: the fact that I was standing on the platform with the rabbi stomping out fires or the thought that all my friends had left me alone up there.

When I finally got back to my seat with my family, I asked my mom, "Do you think anyone noticed?"

LISA CANIS REYNOLDS CHATTANOOGA, TN

THOUGHT TO REMEMBER A gift from the heart lasts forever.

LUMBER MAN "I told my son Chuck that if he wanted a Christmas tree, it was his turn to go out into the woods and cut one down. He was ready and willing," says Robert Siple Sr. of Central Bridge, New York. "The photo was snapped in December 1970, when we lived in a country area outside of Middleburgh, New York."

A YUMMY TRADITION "While our two boys were growing up, in the '60s, they always enjoyed the Hanukkah festivities, especially eating the traditional potato pancakes known as latkes," writes Wille Peters, Albuquerque, New Mexico. "Not even the beautiful candle-lighting ceremony with our family singing, the presents or my elaborate attempts at Hanukkah decorations could distract them from their favorite holiday treat."

THE FAB FIVE "This slide was taken after Christmas of 1964 when the Schiltz kids of Altamont, New York, took up their instruments," writes their mother, Betty Spadaro of Henderson, Nevada. "Our family band included (from left) Donna, 8; Jim, 2; Stephen, 7; Chuck, 3; and Jody, 4." It looks as if a few of the "Beatles" got a dye job, plastic-style.

▲ THAT'S A MOUTHFUL!
"Aunt Mary knew just what to buy for her eight nieces and nephews for Christmas in 1948," says Norman Middleton of Beech Grove, Indiana. "The faces of my sisters and brothers show their joy in every lick of their all-day caramel suckers. Pictured, from the left, are Raymond, Walter, Boyd, Audrey, Doloris, James, me and John."

▲ IS IT MY TURN YET?
"Our sons, Kevin (middle) and Gregory, wait patiently as their dad, Walter Mohr, puts Kev's train together at Christmas 1963," writes Barbara Mohr, Millington, Michigan. "I accidentally bought slide film on our honeymoon in '56—the start of many slide shows."

THOUGHT TO REMEMBER ▸ Show me a squirrel's nest and I'll show you a nutcracker suite.

ORNAMENTAL JEWELRY Sandy Spangler, 8, and her sister, Janice, 4, decided to dress up for Christmas 1954 by decorating themselves, along with the tree, in this slide shared by their father, John, from Hanover, Pennsylvania. "The photo was taken at our home in East Greenville," says John. "The girls were having a good time helping us decorate."

BET A PENNY (FARTHING) ON THE SOX "That's me on the penny-farthing bicycle in 1959 with co-workers Dan Brown (left) and Carl Kunath," says Bud Kilgore, Hillside, Illinois. "The three of us were running up and down Chicago's State Street, 'that great street,' in front of the Sears, Roebuck store, telling everyone to be sure to stop in for a free White Sox ribbon."

CHAPTER 10

Just for Fun

CHEESE! HERE'S A GOOFY GALLERY OF
COMICAL SNAPSHOTS GUARANTEED TO PUT
A GREAT BIG GRIN ON YOUR FACE AND A
LASTING SMILE IN YOUR HEART

Lookin' Good
YOU MUST BE PUTTING US ON!

BOYS BECAME GIRLS FOR '34 SCHOOL PLAY

The teachers at Daniel Bagley Grade School in Seattle decided that the 1934 spring open house needed something fresh and different to get the parents excited about attending.

They hit upon the idea of a play, but not an ordinary one.

"Russell, how would you like to be the mother in the play?" one teacher asked me. In those days, a question like that from a teacher was taken as a direct order.

Several other seventh- and eighth-grade boys were recruited to perform *Mrs. Sniggles and Her Daughters*. The catch? We all would have to wear dresses. In the photo, I'm the one standing.

I took home the 20 pages of script that had my lines. The other boys were rounded up to play my "daughters," but none of us asked how we had been chosen for this dubious honor.

Our pals at school didn't tease us, which we thought was nice of them. Later, we learned the teachers had told the other boys that if they were caught roasting us, they would be added to the cast as more daughters, simply for decorative purposes.

As I introduced my daughters during the performance, each of them had a few lines to say. Some recited a poem, while others told of their lives as daughters in the Sniggles family.

The play turned out to be a great hit, and our parents were surprised at how pretty we looked in girls' clothing, although I'd have to say the fathers were more aghast than surprised.

When I was in high school, I was asked to play Mrs. Sniggles again, with a different group of daughters. The second time around was easier and I really enjoyed the part.

RUSS ARWINE TUKWILA, WA

AIN'T WE CUTE? "This is my favorite picture of my mother, Lela Norris (first row, second from left), and her sister, Vada (first row, second from right)," says Joan Jones of Knoxville, Illinois. "The 'little girl party' in 1925 was attended by the young women who worked at the Monmouth, Illinois, telephone company. They held regular parties and this time dressed as little girls."

REMEMBER STANLEY HOME PARTIES? Some might call this pinch of '50s fun a bit homely, writes Reba Lacey of Lexington, Kentucky. "This wacky snapshot was taken in 1950, when Stanley Home Parties were all the go here in Lexington," she adds. "The unusual hats we're wearing were made from kitchen items. We had parties nearly every week in different ladies' homes, and all of us were well supplied with Stanley Home Products. I'm in front on the right."

THOUGHT TO REMEMBER ➤ Enjoy life…this is not a dress rehearsal.

BE STILL! ➤

"I remember being told by my dad as I got my first haircut, like the boy at right, 'Be still or you'll get your ears clipped off,'" says Al Bowman, Jacksonville, Florida. "I must have done all right, because I don't recall even a nick."

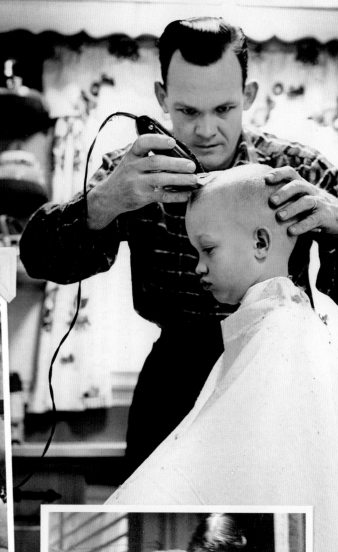

▲ IN THE FLESH

"We gals, all 1947 grads of Hamtramck (Michigan) High, dressed in bathing suits on Christmas Eve," says Irene Lang of Farmington Hills. "In back are Dottie Marko Mallon (left) and Alice Marek. In front, from left, are Loretta Kucab Sobeck, Carol Kozlowski Maloney, me and Barbra Homolka Kohan."

▲ WHAT, NO SHAVE?

"Mom's humor shows in this photo as she gave me a 'haircut' and bath outside our home in rural Luverne, Minnesota, around 1930," says Lily Hartmann of Boulder, Colorado.

▲ ROARIN' GOOD TIME

"My mother, Melita Lips Carpenter (in top hat, bottom row), hosted fun parties in Chicago during the 1920s," says Joan Hill of Wauconda, Illinois. "I think this one had a Roaring Twenties theme."

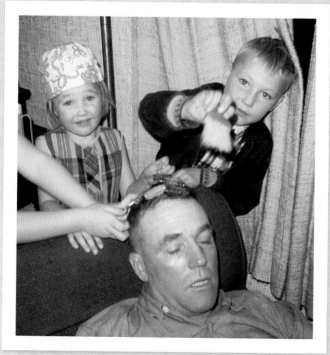

◄ BAD HAIR DAY?

"My father, Paul Schuchmann Jr., liked to rest in his favorite chair at night after a hard day's work on our farm near Arlington, Iowa," writes Sue Becker of Waterloo. "He must have been real tired this night in 1968 when he let me, on the left in my barber's hat, and my brother, Steven, style his hair and even put in a few curlers! My sister, Darla, was also in on the act. Our mother, Bertha, served as our photographer."

Barrels of Fun

RIDING HIGH ON HIJINKS

WHERE THE BOYS ARE

What better way for teenage girls to have some fun than by throwing a slumber party to celebrate a friend's birthday?

I remember a lively, all-night birthday bash, in 1954, for Maggie Byers, who is still one of my best friends. We were all from the Class of '56 at Oakland Technical High School, in Oakland, California.

Someone in our group leaked the party's time and place to the boys we ran around with, so a couple of carloads of boys crashed the party. Were we surprised to see them! Well, we acted that way.

The boys came prepared with their favorite 45 rpm records for an evening of slow dancing. I remember listening to Perry Como, Dean Martin, Frank Sinatra, Nat "King" Cole and Tony Bennett. A few boys brought musical instruments for a potential jam session, hoping the host parents would allow it.

The dancing began, and the festivities got under way. Some of the partyers dashed off to the kitchen to manufacture pizza from a Chef Boyardee kit. Others quietly paired off, looking for some privacy in secluded corners of the house.

When it was nearly midnight, we served birthday cake and ice cream, and the party was officially over. The boys left reluctantly, but much to the relief of the chaperoning parents.

Instead of heading off to sleep, we girls spent those early-morning hours hashing over the evening's events. Who had broken up? Who had fallen in love? Who was going steady? And, most important, whose birthday was coming up so we could start planning our next slumber party?

JUDY A. GOFF CHICO, CA

TKO BY JOE ➤

"My father, Frank Horvath, lost a wager on the Max Schmeling-Joe Louis fight in 1938," says Shirley Tieffenbach of Sussex, Wisconsin. "Joe Louis won that famous bout, so Dad had to wheel the winner of the wager, Russ Rosenwirth, around the Harley-Davidson plant at 37th and Juneau in Milwaukee."

GIDDYUP, POP-POP! "My sons, Danny and Timmy, always enjoyed a ride on their favorite 'horse'–my dad, Russell Boyer," writes Lois Havill, Woodstock, Vermont. "This 1965 photo reminds me of how Dad's strong back bore many burdens of life, while his face and heart smiled."

NO IFS OR ANDS, JUST BUTTS. "This is me in a pushing contest with a buck sheep in 1934," writes J. Gordon Hollis from Waterloo, Iowa. "I was 20 and had many pushing contests with this sheep."

"John Patrick was already 31 hefty pounds at 6 months old when I took this picture of my mother holding him. Mom was barely 5 feet tall and all of 90 pounds. She was unable to lift him, but a grandmother's arms are meant to hold, so she kept him close on her lap."

MAUREEN REID LITTLE SILVER, NJ

THOUGHT TO REMEMBER ➤ Love makes the world go round, but laughter keeps us from getting dizzy.

Let the Good Times Roll

These sidesplitting examples of wacky transportation clearly demonstrate that it's not the destination, it's the journey—and that getting there is half the fun!

Giving her a lift home.

▲ PEDAL, BROTHER

"I'm not sure when this photo of my father, James Mitchell, and his sister, Catherine, was taken, but it looks as if they were having the time of their lives," says James Mitchell Jr. of Rochester, Pennsylvania. "Dad, who was born in 1904, later owned the J.S. Mitchell Bus Co. in New Brighton, Pennsylvania. Aunt Catherine earned a PhD in chemistry and taught for 37 years at Youngstown University in Youngstown, Ohio."

▲ **JOINED AT THE FORK**
"My father, Oliver Dougherty Jr. (right), and his friend Ray Sutter welded their bicycles together in 1937 or '38 and rode the result from Philadelphia to Gettysburg, 160 miles away," says Gail Clement of Sticklerville, New Jersey. "My dad was 16 or 17 at the time."

◄ **ONE-PIG OPEN SLEIGH**
"My mother's brothers (from left), Frank, Tony and John Kulhanek, are pictured in 1916 with a special snowmobile for winter fun on the family farm near Chesaning, Michigan," writes Patricia Bannick of Dimondale. "Their transportation got 27 miles to a gallon of garbage!"

A REALLY BIG SHOE

I wonder how many people recall a giant shoe, made by Endicott-Johnson Shoe Co. workers in 1930, that was a parade favorite in upstate New York's Triple Cities—Endicott, Binghamton and Johnson City—until World War II. Shortly after the 250-pound leather shoe was made, this photo was taken of it and the Grassi family, since nearly all the Grassi adults worked in EJ shoe factories. My dad is the baby in the photo.

The novelty item sank into obscurity before Joseph Monticello Jr., a young EJ employee, found it in 1965 in an abandoned warehouse. Joe restored it and used it as a sales prop. The next year, he joined the Army and headed to Vietnam, leaving the shoe with his parents. His younger siblings played with it until his return from overseas in 1968.

In 1985, Joe passed the prop to an older brother and nephew. The next year, it ended up in a Florida museum, and later was stashed away in Orlando.

The shoe resurfaced in 2010, when Joe's brother learned that Amos Patterson Museum officials wanted to display it. Today, the shoe—restored by a team of cobblers—has a home in an EJ legacy exhibit at the museum in Endicott, New York.

THERESE GRASSI KLEMPKA PORT CRANE, NY

LITTLE BITTY BOWLING "My uncle Lou Loesch was head of Loesch's Sporting Club in Newark, New Jersey," says Ann Pitt from Mountainside. "He sent out these penny postcards to members. This one was mailed in 1912. It looks as if he was quite the kidder, with those little bowling pins and ball and that rough 'alley.'"

LAKESIDE LEVITY "A group from our church took a Sunday drive to this lake in northern Wisconsin in the summer of 1952," writes Bob Crawford of Apple Valley, Minnesota. "I took the slide of the gang and my 1950 Lincoln convertible. I was about 21 years old at the time and working as a printer's apprentice. I believe that I was probably courting one of the young ladies in the car."

ON THE BOARDWALK "My great-aunt Millie Burtner (above, wearing the hat) and her friend Hanna Sovy posed behind a cutout on the Boardwalk in Santa Cruz, California," says Barbara Kling of San Francisco. "I think the photograph was taken sometime in the '50s. Aunt Millie was rarely seen without a hat."

THOUGHT TO REMEMBER ~ Smiles never go up in price or down in value.

"As Dad bent over to start our outboard motor one day in 1956, this little tarpon jumped into our boat and smacked his back," says David Aldridge Jr. of New Hope, Alabama. "At first he thought I was hitting him with an oar!"

PHONY REFRESHERS ►

"Pictured in this photo from Christmas Day 1945 are (front, from left) Tony Licata, Phil Martorana and my dad, Salvatore Alaimo, all age 12; and (back, from left) Peter Vaccaro, 9, and Carmen Martorana, 7," writes Sam Alaimo of Tonawanda, New York. "These lifelong friends were at the penny arcade next to the Alibi tavern at Main and Chippewa streets in downtown Buffalo, stopping for a quick 'refresher' on their way to catch the 5 p.m. war movie at Shea's Buffalo Theatre."

▲ CATCH OF THE DAY
Looks as though this "fisherwoman" is just about to land a big one. The photograph was taken in California in 1958 by Doris Nichols of Mena, Arkansas. The "fish" is actually her son, Mark, who was always clowning around. Doris' niece Karen has the fishing pole.

▲ STEADY, NOW
"My son Rick (left) and his cousin Bill Mitton somehow persuaded Bill's little brother, Tom, to pose for this photo at the home of their grandparents John and Lora Mitton in Albia, Iowa," says Eva Bettis of Leesburg, Florida. "Their makeshift bows may look authentic—but believe me, the arrows wouldn't have gone anywhere."

◄ AT ARM'S LENGTH
Taking a good, long look at herself in a fun-house mirror is Andria Diehl of Azusa, California. The distorting glass—making viewers look short and boxy or tall and skinny—was a classic attraction at carnivals and arcades like this one in the '20s.

Animal Antics

The animal kingdom is chock-full of comedians. And when a camera captures their horseplay and monkey business, the outcome can be absolutely laughable.

MONKEYSHINES "This is my brother, Jack Lucas, with his dapper 'caddy' from the Mack Sennett Studio in 1923," writes Patricia Kane of Las Vegas. "Jack made eight two-reeler movies for Sennett's company, which was known for slapstick comedy."

"BUSING" A BOVINE "In 1949, my dad, Carl (at the wheel), and his brothers Howard (center) and Jack (in glasses) found a deal on a cow they couldn't pass up," says Bob Snyder, Etna, New York. "Not wanting to rent a truck, they chauffeured Bessie home in Dad's Jeep Suburban."

KIDS WILL BE KIDS "We were visiting the San Diego Zoo in 1961 when I set up to take a picture of this goat standing on a large turtle," writes Elmer Nielson of Burbank, California. "Our son Kurt moved up to pet the turtle, and the goat started to lick his hair. This lasted only a split-second, so I was fortunate to record the situation, which my wife, Alice, and I still laugh about."

PLAYFUL PUP "In 1949, my husband, Don, was a lieutenant in the Navy, stationed in Pensacola," writes Phyllis Heberling of Virginia Beach, Virginia. "We rented a house nearby, where I stayed with our 3-year-old, Paul, and awaited the birth of our second child. The antics of our dog, Peoria (tickling the ivories above), kept me from feeling lonely."

THOUGHT TO REMEMBER ➤ Don't judge; you can't tell how far a frog can jump just by looking at it.

SHORT-DISTANCE CALL "In 1965, my wife and I were hysterical with laughter when we spied our sons using walkie-talkies at such a close range," says Irwin Almer of Riverhead, New York. "We sat them down to explain the devices' usefulness and long-distance capability."

My Own Memories